Social Marketing

Secrets and Hacks Top Influencers Use to Grow Their Personal Brand and Business Using Facebook Advertising, Instagram and YouTube

Written By Mark Hollister

This eBook is provided with the sole purpose of providing relevant information on a specific topic for which every reasonable effort has been made to ensure that it is both accurate and reasonable. Nevertheless, by purchasing this eBook you consent to the fact that the author, as well as the publisher, are in no way experts on the topics contained herein, regardless of any claims as such that may be made within. As such, any suggestions or recommendations that are made within are done so purely for entertainment value. It is recommended that you always consult a professional prior to undertaking any of the advice or techniques discussed within.

This is a legally binding declaration that is considered both valid and fair by both the Committee of Publishers Association and the American Bar Association and should be considered as legally binding within the United States.

Additionally, the information in the following pages is intended only for informational purposes and should thus be thought of as universal. As befitting its nature, it is presented without assurance regarding its prolonged validity or interim quality. Trademarks that are mentioned are done without written consent and can in no way be considered an endorsement from the trademark holder.

Table of contents

Introduction

Social media marketing is a necessity in today's online economy. With social media platforms like Facebook, YouTube and Instagram getting millions upon millions of visits each day, there's never been a better time to get involved with social media marketing.

In this book, we'll be covering the essentials of using Facebook and Instagram to promote your business. In addition, we'll also be taking an in-depth look at how to build a YouTube channel that will absolutely explode with growth.

If you've ever wanted to learn the time-tested methods that top social media markers use to generate income and traffic for their businesses, then this is the book for you. We'll look at ways that you can:

- Create strong relationships with your followers

- Build a function sales funnel that has a high conversion rate
- Create quality YouTube content that engages and inspires your audience
- Make Instagram Story ads that grabs attention
- And much, much more!

Chapter 1: Social Media Starters

Throughout the course of this book, we'll be focusing on three of the biggest social media platforms, Facebook, YouTube, and Instagram. However, this chapter is going to be dedicated to the principles of how to properly use social media across the board. These principles can apply to any one of these social media platforms and are necessary if you want to find success in growing your businesses through social media marketing.

The Essentials of Posting on Social Media

Regardless of the type of social media platform that you're using, there are some universal principles to pay attention to when it comes to posting. The first and most important thing to remember is what's known as the 80/20 rule. 80% of what you post should be focused on providing value for your followers, and 20% should be self-promotion.

Why is this? Simply put, people don't care about what you have to sell them. The average person sees hundreds, if not thousands of advertisements a day. If they come across a social media post promoting some kind of product or business, chances are they won't have any interest.

However, if what you are posting provides value to their lives in some way, such as making them laugh or teaching them useful facts, they will be more likely to engage with you. They may like your post, share it with their friends or even follow your page. You may not have advertised directly to them, but by providing a post that isn't about yourself, you've been able to create a connection. Now, later on, when you post a self-promotion post, they may be more interested in listening to you.

The 80/20 rule is about to give and take. You want to give your followers on social media as many valuable posts a possible. Your posts should educate, entertain or inspire others. Then, every now and then, you share a little post selling your products, or linking to your website. This self-promotion, when done in moderation, will be tolerated.

Think about social media like a conversation. No one wants to talk to someone who only talks about themselves. Instead, they want to talk with someone who is willing to go back and forth, sharing value about multiple topics. Amateur social media marketers make the mistake of thinking that social media posting is all about promoting a product. In fact, this isn't quite right. Instead, social media posting is about connecting to followers and promoting a brand. By following the 80/20 rule, you are increasing the chances of fan engagement, and decreasing the chances of being unfollowed on Facebook!

What to Share?

Sharing is the core of most social media outlets. Platforms like Facebook, Twitter, and Instagram, are all about sharing different pictures, ideas, and concepts with one another. As a business, you need to know what to share and what not to. Sometimes the wrong kind of post can significantly hurt your reputation.

Ideally, the best types of content to share is original content that you have created. Infographics, funny pictures, custom made memes and graphics that have been watermarked can quickly grow popular and be circulated around. Visual content is one of the most valuable types of content that you can post, as most people are looking for pictures, not blocks of text when they start endlessly scrolling through Facebook.

Of course, creating custom content takes time and work. You can also report other people's content, as long as you give proper credit to the source. This is an excellent practice with specific platforms, such as Twitter, where sharing content is often reciprocated. Just make sure that if you are reposting or sharing other's content that you are giving credit where it is due. The last thing you want is to end up being the target of a frustrated creator who thinks you were ripping them off.

There are some things that you will want to avoid when posting on social media. Offensive images, political statements, and poorly made memes are all something that should be left behind. Some posters might think that using their business to promote a political idea might attract more customers, but oftentimes this backfires in some way. The best position is to simply stay apolitical when posting through your own business social media pages. The internet is just too polemic for politics, especially if it could affect your bottom line.

Creating an effective profile:

When it comes to social media, profiles are extremely important. They contain the whole of your brand identity. When a follower comes across your social media profile, they will be learning a lot about you in a single glance. You'll need to make sure that your profile looks visually appealing and conveys the proper information to viewers.

The first step to making good profiles across the board is to have a strong brand identity that is uniform. This means that regardless of which platform a follower is using, they can expect you to have the same logo as well as banners. This helps to create a cohesive image and lets viewers know that you are serious business. Keep descriptions the same across the board as well, quickly informing viewers about your company, your goals, and your values.

Another important thing to take note of when creating your profiles is that this account is purely for professional purposes. This doesn't mean that you can't be personal and authentic with people, but it does mean that you will want to treat your profile professionally. Make sure that you don't have any unprofessional images or posts in your history. Don't try to convert your personal social media profiles into business ones. Instead, make a fresh profile that doesn't have any of the baggage from a personal account.

Stay Professional

Professionalism is the key to running an excellent social media account. Regardless of the platform that you are running, you should strive, above all else, to keep your company in good standing in the eyes of others. The memory of the internet is a long one. Once you post something online, it's going to be out there forever. You might not think it, but if you make a heated decision to put something inflammatory on your personal account, there is a guarantee that someone will take a screenshot of it. Don't cost your business customers by acting in an unprofessional manner. Stay confident with others, avoid polemic and political subjects and above all, respect everyone in the conversation. As long as you keep your head above water, you won't have to worry about being targeted on social media by people who are angry at you for what you have said. Be polite, respectful and careful. Remember, when it comes to social media, everyone really is watching you.

The Difference Between Marketing and Advertising

Social media marketing has opened up quite a bit of opportunity for those businesses who are trying to make money online. Yet, oftentimes a marketer is sabotaged by the fact that they can't quite tell the difference between marketing and advertising. These words aren't interchangeable; in fact, they have very separate meanings.

Marketing refers to all of the efforts that you undertake to promote your company and your brand. When you make a post on social media, even if it's unrelated to selling your products, it is marketing. When you talk to a few friends about your new company, that also is marketing.

Advertising, on the other hand, is a subset of marketing. It is a type of marketing that has a particular definition. To advertise, you are paying money in order to promote your products, often with the hopes of getting direct conversions. So advertising is a form of marketing, but marketing is not advertising.

Social media marketing, therefore, is not merely just about paying money to buy ads. Instead, it is about performing all of the other types of marketing out there. Customer support, prospecting, creating relationships and generating buzz are all that the social media component allows for. Your focus, when working on social media, shouldn't only be about selling your products. Rather it should be about creating a sense of community with those who are interested in your company.

The good news about social media is that you can both market and advertise at the same time. Platforms like Facebook have some of the most potent advertising systems in the world, allowing you to find and target the right kind of customers. The trick is to keep a wall of separation between the two efforts. Advertising is a paid endeavor; you spend money in order to promote and sell your products. Marketing is creating a community and promoting your products in an organic manner.

Choosing the Right Platform:

While most principles of social media are universal, meaning they apply regardless of the platform being used, this doesn't mean every platform is the same. Facebook, YouTube, Instagram, Twitter, and SnapChat are all vastly different from one another. One of the challenges most social media marketers face is figuring out which of these platforms to use. Some might want to compound their efforts by simply choosing to use all of them, but this can be somewhat of an exhausting task. Rather than focusing on every type of social media platform out there, try to single out two or three that you feel would be best for you.

So what should you consider when choosing your preferred platforms to be working with? The first and foremost is your target demographic. Certain platforms work better with certain age groups. For example, Instagram and Snapchat tend to skew towards the younger demographics. Facebook appeals to pretty much any age across the board.

After age, you'll need to consider interest. Is there a vast number of people in your target interest group that use these platforms? Spend some time searching through the platform, look at the search results for niche specific keywords, as well as the hashtags. If you can't find a vast number of individuals talking about those subjects, you'll most likely want to use a different social media platform.

And of course, after you have age and interest determined, consider your own proficiency with the platform. If you are comfortable and well versed with a platform, then you should probably focus on using that as your first choice. Remember, part of social media is consistency. You'll need to be making multiple posts a week. If you personally don't care for using a specific type of social media platform, then you most likely will shy away from using it. Try to use the ones that you enjoy, so that you have extra motivation when it comes to making your weekly posts.

What are the best platforms to use?

While every platform has its own value and unique range of options, not all are created equal. The biggest platform is currently Facebook which commands the most amount of a social media user's time. YouTube is the runner up, winning second place for the largest social media platform, although it functions almost entirely different from other types of social media. And Instagram comes in a little lower on the charts but has a significantly higher level of engagement with younger consumers. So much so, that a new class of advertising has emerged, known as Instagram Influencers, who are able to shape consumer decisions simply by pitching and endorsing products in their Instagram feeds. We will be covering these three platforms and how to make the most out of each one, starting with Facebook.

Chapter 2: Facebook Essentials

Facebook has plenty of incredible features that will assist you in your social media marketing efforts. And it all starts with the simple creation of your Facebook Business Page. The Facebook Business page is the central hub for you; without one, you cannot run ads, nor can you make posts.

To create a Facebook Business page, all you need is a regular Facebook account. Once you have your account established, you just click on Create Pages. This will take to you to a section where you will be able to fill in all of the necessary details to create the Facebook Page for your business. One crucial step is to make sure that you set up a secure two-layer permission model so that you don't have to worry about security risks.

To set up the two-factor authentication model, you'll need to go to the security and login settings. From there, just select the two-factor authentication feature, which will then prompt Facebook to take you through a series of steps that will increase the protection of your account. Two-factor authentication requires that you have some external way of confirming your identity, usually through phone messaging. This will trigger whenever Facebook detects suspicious activity or if you're logging in on a different device than usual.

Top Features of Facebook

Facebook offers a ton of great features that make it easy for those who wish to implement social media marketing into their business. Let's take a look at the top ten that will allow you to get the most out of your marketing time and energy.

Post Scheduling:

Posting is an important component of using a Facebook page. On average, you are going to want to post at least once a day, five days a week. Posting more than once per day isn't ideal, as Facebook's algorithms don't want to promote business pages that repeatedly post, so make sure you just stick to the one. However, even making one post every single day might seem like quite the task, especially when you consider the time it takes to sit down, think up a post and then actually post it.

Fortunately, Facebook provides you with the necessary tools to plan your posts ahead of time with their scheduling system. All you need to do is create the post, but instead of clicking "publish now" simply select the post later button and begin your scheduling.

In general, you should schedule one or two weeks out at a time. Take a day to work on all of them at once, and then just schedule them out. This will save you valuable time within your week and most importantly, will allow you to create a cohesive content schedule.

Page Likes:

Your business page is a great way to collect data about your customers. The first type of data that you will want to collect merely is your potential customer's identities. This can quickly be captured through the use of Page Likes. A customer who has liked your products, your posts or is interested in what you have to say has the option to "Like" your page. Once they have liked your page, they will be able to see your posts in their feed. This gives you access to their social media browsing time without having to contact them directly.

With that in mind, it's important to realize that Page Likes is one of the most important parts of using a Facebook page. You will want to get as many likes from ideal customers as possible. In addition to allowing customers to see your new posts, alike also provides you with an audience that you can use to target during your Facebook ad campaigns.

There are many different ways to gain Facebook likes, but the easiest is clear visibility. You should make a point to refer customers to your Facebook page, either through direct invitation, or having a link on your websites. This can allow for them to like your page quickly. Other methods involve running a campaign through Facebook ads, promoting a post or even your page so you can collect more data.

It's important to remember that while likes are important, not every Page like is created equally. You'll want to make sure that you only solicit likes from potential customers. Don't waste your time trying to swell your page up as much as you can by targeting non-customers. It's not a popularity contest in the least.Low-quality followers won't amount to conversion and can waste your time when trying to create look-alike audiences later on.

How can you avoid low-quality followers? Simple enough, try not to make posts that aren't relevant to your business or your brand.

Branching out might seem like the best way to gain likes, but it's better to keep a tight lid on the type of content that you produce. It's better to attract 10 high-quality followers than 100 low-quality ones.

Insights:

Data collection is one of the most crucial components of social media marketing. You're going to need to collect and interpret data to learn how to target your potential customers better. Facebook provides insights that allow you to see how many people have been visiting your page, who is interacting with what content and what links are most clicked.

It's important to monitor the data on a weekly basis, taking note of how many people are visiting your pages, what content is the most popular, etc. By collecting this data, you'll be able to make decisions about what kind of content you want to continue releasing, and which content you should discontinue. For example, if a type of picture you're sharing has become immensely popular, you will want to make sure that you repost it from time to time, logging that is valuable to your customers. If a post hasn't received much attention or comments, then you should probably look into what it isn't performing as well.

Facebook Business Account:

The Facebook Business account is the central hub for creating advertisements, running them as well as operating multiple pages. If you're looking to get serious about your Facebook page, you're going to need to create a Business account and then link your page to the account. The good news is that Facebook Business is a free service and offers a lot of options.

With the business account, you can access advanced analytics, create additional users and run multiple Facebook pages at once. You can also create varying levels of access for your users, so if you have multiple employees, you can give them advertiser or user access without giving them full control.

Facebook Pixel:

The Facebook pixel is a nifty little feature that you add to your own website. When activated, the Facebook pixel is able to pick up traffic that visits your websites through your Facebook pages and ads. When someone clicks on your Facebook ad and is redirected to your website, the pixel attaches to them and allows for you to retarget them with later marketing. On top of that, you can also set up the pixel to see what kind of actions are being taken by visitors, so you can know which advertising efforts are leading to the most conversions.

Creating a Facebook pixel will require you to create a Facebook Business account first. Once you've made the business account, you just need to go to the tools section and select the Pixel. This will take you through the steps necessary to create your own pixel. You'll need to install the pixel itself on your website. This may take a few more steps, depending on the content management system you're using for your website.

Once you have created the Facebook Pixel, you'll be able to detect the traffic that follows your ads and collect data on them through Facebook. This will increase the specificity of the data you are collecting about your visitors and will give you a better picture of what their behaviors are.

Chatbot Integration:

One of the problems with running a business is that you often cannot answer questions for a customer quickly. They'll have to email or call you and then wait for a response. If you're busy or have a high load of questions from customers, you might not be able to quickly respond as you'd like. However, with Facebook, you can integrate what is known as a Chatbot.

A Chatbot is an automated AI system that is able to provide answers to questions from customers. From their point of view, all they need to do is send you a question via messenger and the chatbot will quickly respond. It will be able to identify keywords and answer most frequently asked questions about the product. The customer is able to get rapid responses to their questions, and you get to make a great impression on them. Best of all, you don't have to actually be there to field their questions.

Facebook allows for chatbot integration on your pages. They don't host the chatbots themselves, as those are third-party applications that will require installation. There are third party companies, such as Chatfuel or Botsify that will provide you with everything necessary to integrate a chatbot on your Facebook page. The only downside is that there is a cost associated with using these third parties. However, if used correctly, a chatbot can significantly increase the chances of getting a sales conversion.

Facebook Groups:

Facebook allows for the creation of what is known as a Group. A group is an invitation based platform where users are able to join and then share content with one another. They are able to talk, share ideas and pictures and operate in their own private little Facebook. Some groups are open, meaning you just need to click join in order to be able to see content and post, while others are set to private or invitation only.

As a marketer, you're going to want to create a Facebook group of your own, most likely surrounding the niche that you are selling it. However, it's important to take note that the purpose of a Facebook group is to create and foster a sense of community, *not* to sell things. This means that if you are going to create or join a group, you should work to be as giving as possible. Share useful content, answer questions, give advice and even ask questions yourself. Foster a healthy dialogue with others. Don't try to market your material in a Facebook group, as this can often be seen as cold and mercenary. Instead, just use groups to create a good community.

When people have gotten to know your brand through a group, it increases the level of trust that they have with you, especially if you have been treating them well. This can increase the chances of them converting organically. On top of that, being a part of a group gives you access to the thoughts and opinions of people in your target demographic. You can use this information to aid you in your advertising efforts later on. In fact, you can even use these groups to aid you in product development for the future. If you take note of what people want and then give it to them, you'll be able to generate sales at a much faster rate than if you were to have no feedback at all.

Creating and joining multiple Facebook groups is a good idea. If your company has a large enough customer base for it, you might want to consider creating a Facebook group about your own products. This is another excellent way to allow your customers to talk to you about their concerns or questions directly. Plus, when they are in a group specifically for your own company, you are free to promote your products without it seeming crass or inappropriate. After all, everyone expects a company to promote their stuff in their own spaces.

Call To Action Button:

One feature that you can't miss when building your Facebook page is the call to action button. This button, found on the righthand corner of the screen, is what will help move your customers closer to taking the action that you want them to take. Facebook has a list of different actions that you can list, such as Buy Now. These buttons are then hyperlinked with a link of your choice. All the potential customer has to do is click on that link, and then they'll go to wherever you direct them.

It's essential to have a simple call to action button that reflects the ultimate goal of your Facebook page. If you want them to visit your website, if you want to sell a product or if you just want to get them to email you, you'll need to incorporate that into the Call to Action button. However, you only get one, so make sure that whichever call to action that you want to incorporate in your button is the most pivotal one. Remember, the goal of any kind of sales funnel is to reduce the number of steps necessary to convert. You don't want your customer having to click through 9+ links in order to make a purchase. Try to keep it as simple as possible. We'll talk more about the creation of a sales funnel in the next chapter.

Facebook Stories:

Facebook stories are a newer feature that allows for users and Facebook pages to create short, 24 hour long stories. These stories contain both video and pictures, which you can use to share with viewers. They don't last long but allow followers to get a glimpse into the world for your business. You can create behind the scenes stories, unique event stories or even tell personal stories with Facebook Stories.

The drawback behind Facebook stories is that you'll need to spend time planning out how you want your story to play out. You'll need to take the photos and the videos, then work on stringing them together into a functional narrative. However, if you are able to do so, Facebook stories can create a stronger connection with viewers. A stronger connection means they might engage more with your company as well as your posts.

Pinning Posts:

First impressions are extremely important when it comes to social media. You're going to need to make the best possible impression on visitors as quickly as possible. Attention is in short supply, especially when you consider how much the internet has to offer. One great way to capture attention is to use Facebook's pinned post system. Facebook allows for you to pin a single post, from anywhere on your timeline, at the very top of your Facebook page.

This allows viewers to see your best content immediately upon clicking your Facebook page. Look for the post that has made the biggest impression with others, or looks for one that has some kind of enticing offer, such as a business deal that you're currently running. By pinning a post, you can quickly capture attention. Once that attention has been captured, the visitor will hopefully begin to scroll through your content. If they like what they see, they'll like the page or better yet, visit your website!

Chapter 3: Creating the Avatar

All of your marketing efforts are meant to target specific individuals, individuals who have the greatest chance of purchasing your products. Your target demographic is known as an avatar. An avatar is a representation of your ideal customer. If you want to be able to sell products online, you've got to be able to identify your avatar first.

Creating the Avatar:

An avatar is a picture, a snapshot of the type of customer who would most likely make the purchase. In order to create the avatar, you need to determine their habits, their age, their gender as well as their hobbies and interests.

You must work to create as specific an avatar as possible because once you begin your efforts with Facebook advertising, you'll want to know what kind of behavior you want to target.

Let's take a look at how to create the avatar, step by step.

Step One: Identify the primary gender

Different genders make different purchasing decisions. When creating the avatar, you'll need to research on average, which gender engages with your product the most. This will help much when it comes to customizing your ads and determining which kind of content to create.

Identifying the primary gender takes time and research. If you have access to Google analytics, you should be able to determine rather quickly which group engages the most with your products. You can also do market research, to specify this even more.

This doesn't mean that you aren't going to be marketing to both genders, however. Some products or niches tend to skew close to the middle. If that's the case, then that's great news, you have a unisex product! However, certain niches are just quite simply going to be dominated by one specific gender. It's good to have that data figured out so you can custom your marketing efforts later on.

Step Two: Identify the avatar's age

Age is another critical piece of the puzzle. Facebook's metrics allow you to target specific age groups, so it is imperative that you do the research to determine what the age of your avatar can range from. For example, you don't want to say "this product appeals to young women," rather you would want to say "This product appeals to women between ages 18-25." The more specific data you can gain on the age groups interested in your product or niche, the better.

Step Three: Identify the avatar's interests

While it is evident that your avatar would be interested in your product, you should also look at other behaviors and interests that exist parallel to your niche. For example, if you are selling fishing gear, you might want to look into other interests and behaviors that fisherman engage in, such as hiking, camping or boating. By identifying these behaviors, you'll be able to not only create more relevant ads, but you will also be able to specifically target people who engage in these behaviors.

Make a list of all the interests and hobbies your avatar has. Then, create sublists underneath those hobbies and interests, to see what subcategories can exist. This will take time and research but will give you a better picture of what kind of person you are selling to.

Step Four: Create multiple avatars

You don't need only one avatar. Rather, you just need one avatar per advertising campaign. As a practice, you should be able to extract multiple types of avatars from your product or service. There are always multiple types of customers who have a need for your product. By dividing these customers into categories, separating them based off of things like age, interest, and gender, you'll be able to create avatar profiles of each group.

Then, as you work on your marketing and advertising efforts, you can run specific campaigns targeting specific avatars. This will help refine the type of ads you are running. Instead of using just one net to try and capture a bunch of different fish, you can use multiple rods, each with bait custom made for each avatar.

Chapter 4: Facebook Ads

Facebook ads are some of the most powerful forms of advertising on the planet. Few other engines out there allow for you to target specific groups of people, interests, age, and gender, all for the purpose of putting an advertisement directly in front of them. If you use Facebook ads right, you'll generate higher levels of income, increase brand awareness and get the conversions that you've always wanted!

Understanding Audiences:

In Facebook advertising, the audience is one of the most necessary components for running an ad properly. The audience is essentially the target of your advertisements. When you fund and run an ad, Facebook will begin to search for people who meet your audience profiles and then will place the ad in front of them. Hopefully, the audience member will then interact with the ad in some way, either by reading it or clicking on it.

If you've done your homework, you should already have all of the metrics necessary for creating for your audience on Facebook ads. All you need to do is take the interests, ages, behaviors and other metrics from your avatar and then plug them in. This will create the first official audience for your ad run.

However, you aren't finished once you have created your first audience. Over time, the more you run a Facebook ad, you will be able to create a better-defined audience. You'll be able to take your current audience that you have created, find the people who have engaged, put them in their own audience and create what is known as a lookalike.

A lookalike audience is a group of people who have the same interests and preferences as one of your existing audiences. Facebook retrieves these people using algorithms and then stores them as an audience for you so that you can run ads for an entirely new group of people. Even though none of these people have seen or interacted with your ads before, since they are similar to your previous audience, they will be in the most relevant categories.

You can also generate audiences from your email list if you have been creating one. All you need to do is use the import tool from the Facebook Business manager. Then, you'll be able to create another lookalike audience, using the data that Facebook is able to locate these individuals through their own system. This is a great way to generate lookalike audiences if you have a large email list, but you haven't begun advertising through Facebook yet.

Creating Ad Campaigns

Facebook ad campaigns are highly targeted and goal oriented. You, as the marketer, get to choose what kind of goal you are looking to achieve, be it product sales, generating awareness or simply getting people to visit your website and read your content.

The most important part of an ad campaign is determining the effectiveness of each ad that you run. Ads cost money to run. You're going to be paying Facebook a set amount of money per day in order to get your ads placed, although most of the time you only pay when someone actually clicks on your link. Regardless of how you pay, one thing remains clear: you want to pay as little as possible and get as many conversions as possible.

The best way to do this is to work on creating extremely efficient ads. Ads that convert users quickly and that help create a sense of desire within the viewer. A good ad can make all the difference in the world.

What makes a good ad?

Ask ten different marketers what makes a good advertisement and you'll most likely get ten different answers. The truth is that there is no magical formula when it comes to advertising. Sometimes an ad can perform extremely well for no apparent reason, and other times an ad that you sunk a ton of effort into can crash and burn.

This is because until you throw something out on the market to actually test it, you won't really know if an ad will perform well. There are valuable and important principles that you can follow to develop good ad copy, but at the end of the day, all that matters is how the customer is going to respond to those ads.

The good news here is that this means you don't have to worry too much about getting it absolutely right the first time. Experimentation is the name of the game, so you are free to try new and exciting things, testing until you get one that performs exceptionally well.

A good ad is simply an ad that gets conversions. It doesn't matter how much you spent on it, how pretty it looks or how great of a call to action is on the card, if the ad doesn't perform, it's bad and should be discarded.

That being said, there are three essential elements to creating a functional and performing ad. Those elements are copy, design, and call-to-action.

Copy:

A copy is a text used on the ad, both inside of the ad itself and above the ad. These words are quick descriptions of your product and should be meant to inspire curiosity and interest in the customer. In general, you will want to be brief, as you have only a limited amount of space for the wording, as well as a limited amount of attention from the reader.

Design:

The design is the visual portion of the advertisement. This is what will capture the attention of the reader first. Words are helpful, but in reality, graphic design is the most important part of the advertisement. Without a good visual design, most people will only look past your ad. Remember, people, come across your ads while they are scrolling down. You'll want something eye-popping to catch their interest. If you can create an ad that will make them stop scrolling, even for just a second, you've done an excellent job with your design.

Call to Action:

The call to action should be a short line that pushes the viewer to take a specific action and click on the link. Usually, a call to action is succinct, punchy and prompts the reader to act now, as opposed to later.

What should I spend on ad creation?

If you're just starting out, then you will most likely want to keep costs low. There are plenty of online tools out that there allow you to create your own ads for free. Websites such as Canva allow for you to create high quality, good looking ads without having all of the skills of a graphic designer. This frees you up to experiment a bit, test out what you're thinking about and then when you're ready; you can run the ad.

Conversely, if you've got a larger budget or don't have the creative talent necessary to create a good looking ad, there are options to hire a freelancer through websites such as Fiverr or Upwork. These freelancers will work for a set fee and can create ads that will look great. However, there is no guarantee that spending a lot of money on an ad set will guarantee the ad will perform well. So don't spend too much, try to keep your budget within $5 to $10 per ad and make sure that you get multiple iterations of each ad.

A/B Testing

The real secret to creating a good ad is to test it relentlessly until you are confident that the ad is performing to its full potential. Facebook allows for what is known as A/B testing, where you run two ads at the same time, and then can compare the performance of these ads when you have finished the ad run.

A/B testing is beneficial because it lets you test two ideas for the same price. As you go about your business, running ad campaigns to raise awareness and sell products, you're going to want to keep costs low. A/B testing is the measure that allows you to keep those costs at a minimum.

By running two different ads at the same time, you will be able to measure the performance of each one in detail. You can see which ads converted the most, had the most clicks and generated the most interest. If the ads perform similarly, you can assume that these ads will run together just fine. If things skew in one direction, you can ditch the underperforming ads and focus on the ones that are winners.

You should commit to A/B testing whenever you design new ads. Plan a campaign around testing them for a week or so. Once they have finished their run, you can analyze the numbers and determine what to do next. Make sure that you are testing for a full week at least. The last thing you want to do is skew the numbers by only running the ad for a day or two. You'll need a long enough run to where you can determine if an ad is running reliably and that a spike in conversions and clicks isn't just a fluke.

Different Ads for Different Avatars:

When you created your avatars, you most likely were able to identify at least two different groups of people that would be interested in your products. Rather than simply try to run an ad that targets both groups at the same time, it would be far more efficient to create ads that appeal to each group individually.

Facebook audiences already allow you to create different audience profiles. You can save these audiences and use them as much as you like. This means when you create an ad campaign, you can choose which audience you want to put your ad in front of. So, if you have Avatar A with a different makeup from Avatar B, but you're selling the same products to them, rather than just run one ad for both, why not run two ads for each group?

You can tailor the ad to each of your avatars needs, interests and desires. If you know, for example, that Avatar A wants your product because they need it professionally and Avatar B wants your product because they are hobbyists, you would want to create two ads that appeal to each avatar. This is a highly specific style of advertising, and it works wonders on improving your conversion rates.

Chapter 5: Creating the Sales Funnel

Facebook Ads are powerful tools, but they are just that, a tool. If you want to reach success through your marketing endeavors, you're going to need more than just a tool. You're going to need a process that takes customers from hesitation to purchasing in only a few steps. In other words, you're going to need a sales funnel.

A sales funnel a process that is designed to capture a potential customer's interests and then move them downwards, towards the final process of purchasing. A funnel is made up of several different phases; some of them happen automatically, whereas other phases require action from the customer.

The Sales Funnel Phases:

There are four phases of the sales funnel: awareness, education, decision, conversion. Each one of these steps requires special care and focus, especially if you want to get them down to that final step.

The Awareness Phase:

The awareness phase happens almost instantly. A customer is unaware of your product, and then when you introduce it, they become aware. Either they see an ad in passing, they came across one of your social media posts, or they end up on your website. Regardless of how they come across information about your company or product, the end result is all the same: they now know you exist.

The awareness phase can be rather quick, especially if you aren't careful. Someone can become aware of your product and then for some reason, lose interest. Perhaps they didn't care for the name or claims of the product. Maybe they aren't part of the target demographic or maybe your ad just didn't catch their eye.

The good news is that awareness can be built up over time. A consumer might become only vaguely aware of your product at first, but after a few more advertisements, social media posts or word of mouth endorsements, they may end up becoming aware enough to move onto the next step.

The Education Phase:

Once a customer has become aware enough of the product to become interested in it, they will begin to move into the education phase. This is where they spend the time to learn about the product and how it will provide value to their life. They will perhaps read about it on your website, look for product reviews, analyze the data and then move onto the third phase.

You must be prepared to educate the consumer as much as possible. You should do everything in your power to make your website easy to navigate, full of useful information and user-friendly so that they don’t struggle to access that information. Your job is to help the customer come to the conclusion that the product would be perfect for them.

In the online world of business, most customers are quite discerning. They will spend a great deal of time doing the research to determine whether a product is worth it or not. Why? Because for the most part, consumers are rather savvy. They want the best deal possible for the lowest price possible. Your job is to find ways to speed up the research process and create a rapport with them so that they look at you as credible.

One of the most effective ways to aid customers in the education phase is to have a review system in place. Reviews are considered to be one of the most trusted ways for a consumer to make a decision. The first thing most consumers look at is the review or star rating of a product. If the ratings are high, then they know that they are making a good purchase and it will put them at ease. Most importantly, if the reviews are especially good, it will generate excitement in the consumer which may lead them to make a purchasing decision.

The Decision Phase:

After a customer has evaluated the product and educated themselves enough on it, they will enter the decision phase. This is the most crucial phase because it is the moment where they decide to make the purchase, decline to buy anything or just say to themselves "not yet."

If a customer decides that they want to make the purchase, they will immediately go into the final phase and begin converting. This, of course, is the ideal situation. You'll want to have worked hard enough in the first two phases to where the decision to make the purchase is easy and quick for the consumer. After some time and energy, they'll say to themselves "I want this!" and will go for it.

While you may have a few direct conversions, the bulk of the people who move through your funnel are going to decline to make the purchase. Their decision will be a solid “no.” The only problem here is that we don’t know the reason why they said no. There are a wide variety of factors that could lead to a consumer declining to make the purchase.

The first and most immediate reason is financial. Not everyone has the money to make the purchase at the exact moment that they have evaluated their product. This can be both a blessing and a curse. A blessing in the sense that you haven't lost them quite yet, a curse because it can pose a problem in getting them to remember your product later on when they have the money to make the purchase.

Others reasons for declining might include being distracted from making the purchase, losing interest in the product, deciding to wait for a sale or wanting to buy it, but some other factor such as high shipping discouraged them from making the sale.

These reasons can all cut into your bottom line, but they don't quite signal that the customer is completely lost yet. This is why you should always make a point to run retargeting ads on people who have visited your site but haven't made a purchase. Just because someone doesn't make the purchase right then and there doesn't necessarily mean they never will. By using retargeting methods, such as the Facebook pixel, you will be able to get your product back in front of them at a later date. If something in their life has changed, or if they had simply gotten distracted and clicked away before buying, you can give them a reminder.

Once you have run a retargeting ad, you'll be able to determine if these previous individuals have indeed declined or not. If they interact with your ad, perhaps in the hopes of getting some kind of bargain you are offering, then all hope is not lost! They will most likely convert at some point, if not today, someday in the future.

However, if they don't engage with your retargeting ad, then you will most likely have lost them. They have chosen to exit the funnel, simply because they have decided to decline to make the purchase at all. The truth about marketing is that while you can get a product in front of a person, you simply cannot force them to make the purchase. As the old adage goes, "you can lead a horse to water, but you can't make him drink." No amount of clever copywriting, salesmanship or flashy tactics can force a person to pull the trigger on the purchase. If they have decided against making the purchase because they don't like or want the product, there is little you can do to persuade them otherwise.

The Conversion Phase:

The final phase of the sales funnels the most exciting one: the conversion phase! This is where the customer takes all of the actions necessary to convert to the behavior that you want them to engage in. Most commonly, this would be them making a purchase, signing up for your email list, subscribing to your Patreon, etc.

The conversion phase should be quick and effortless. If you give the customer too much time to think things over or make the conversion process too convoluted, they may end up abandoning ship before they make the purchase. Some customers might get too frustrated to even work with you again, especially if you suddenly spring hidden charges on them or change the nature of the deal once they almost finished checking out.

The number of steps required to convert should be monitored very closely. Try to get your customer from the start to the finish line in a few steps as possible. Remove every barrier possible so that they can cross through that line and make the purchase as quickly as possible. This is a win-win situation for the both of you, they get a product or service they want, and you get a conversion!

Using Facebook To Make a Sales Funnel

Facebook and Facebook advertising provides you with all of the things you need to create your own sales funnel process. If you want to make a sales funnel that has a high conversion rate, then there are some principles that you need to embrace. Let's take a look at each of these principles in detail.

Principle One: Conversion is the last step, not the first

Let's face it, anyone who is marketing something wants to see the conversion. Regardless of what that conversation is, be it a sale or signup, we all want to see the conversion rate surge to the highest point possible. And since we're looking for conversions, we tend to judge the effectiveness of our sales funnels and marketing efforts based on the amount of conversion we get with initial ad runs.

However, if you look at the shape of the sales funnel, conversion is the last step, not the first. If you want to get a high conversion rate, then you're going to have laid down the groundwork. This means you'll need to focus on building awareness for your potential customers first. And it means you'll also need to be spending both advertising and marketing efforts to increase that awareness.

Think of awareness as planting seeds. If a farmer wants to be a successful farmer, they don't just plant one seed and hope to see that they can get a huge tomato that will feed the entire family. Instead, they plant as many seeds as they are able, spreading them out so that they are able to get a bigger haul during the harvest. A single conversion is excellent, but it's not the end-all be-all.

Rather, you will want to work to create concrete strategies that not only increase awareness in your target demographic but also brings the awareness levels higher each time they come in contact with those ads. Most people breeze past an advertisement on the first viewing.

But the second, third or fourth time? If the ads are doing their job, it will create a higher level of awareness that will move them into the second phase.

As you work to build your funnel, remember that conversions are the harvest. You still need to plant, nurture and tend to your fields until you are able to reap what you have sewn.

Principle Two: Capture Leads

Once you have generated enough awareness to get a consumer to begin engaging with an ad or post on your Facebook page, you should work to capture their information, so that you can market to them later on. The easiest way to do this is through the creation of what is known as a lead magnet.

A lead magnet is something that convinces a potential lead to give you their email address, in exchange for some kind of free, relevant gift. Capturing the email address of a prospect is extremely important, as it will allow you to work to retain them if they decide against making the conversion right now.

For those who decline to make the conversion during the third phase of the sales funnel, a quick email reminding them about your product or offering a special deal can be enough to convince them to come back. And for those who plan on converting but will do so at a later date, a few emails here and there will constantly remind them all about your products.

Facebook has powerful tools for lead generation, allowing for you to gain email signups from those who are interested in your products or brand. These first ads are one of the types of ads that you can run from the Facebook Ads Manager. They will allow customers to directly sign up for your mailing list, often in exchange for some kind of product.

Lead magnets are really the secret weapon for capturing these emails. If you want to run a serious ad campaign, then you absolutely need to develop a lead magnet so that you can generate high-quality leads. This has two benefits, the first we've already mentioned, retargeting. The second benefit is that you can market directly to interested customers inbox without having to pay a third party for marketing. So ultimately, a lead magnet will save you money in the long run.

What should your lead magnet be? As a rule of thumb, the lead magnet should be a gift that is valuable enough to motivate the prospect to share their email in exchange for it. However, you should also take care to make sure that your lead magnet isn't valuable enough to generate interest from people outside of your target demographic. If that's the case, you might end up getting a ton of emails from people who will never convert.

In general, the lead should be something easy to give away and something that costs you very little. Most of the time, a free eBook is one of the best types of lead magnets. As long as the eBook contains valuable information that the consumer can use, it will most likely convert. If you're primarily selling physical products, then discount codes, free shipping or other such products that help motivate the consumer to make the purchase are a good idea.

Regardless of what you choose the lead magnet to be, it simply has to be attractive. Once you have figured out the right kind of bait to use, all you need to do is spend time advertising for it. Over time, you'll find that you'll generate quite a bit of email through this. The best part is that these emails are composed primarily of warm or hot leads, leads that have interacted with you enough to prove that they take action. From there, you can start your own campaign, emailing your prospects and leading them further along your sales funnel.

Principle Three: Facebook is not the end step

Facebook is great. As a social media platform, there are so many different features and options that they offer; you'd be crazy not to use them. However, Facebook is not the end step for the conversion process. The features and tools that Facebook offers are great for you to make initial contact with customers. But once you have made contact, you'll want to move them further along the funnel, and part of that movement involves moving them away from Facebook and towards your own websites.

Why? Simply put, Facebook only offers you a small fraction of the customer's attention. They still have their messenger bugging them, notifications, recommendations and a feed that will steal hours from them if they aren't careful. You don't have their full attention when they're on Facebook. As part of your awareness funnel, you will want to work to develop a method that will move them away from Facebook to a website where you have the ability to command their full attention.

Generally, these websites are referred to as landing pages. A landing page is a dedicated webpage designed simply to focus on one and only one thing: the product, service or brand you are selling. A landing page is designed to take customers through all four steps of the sales funnel, from start to finish.

The landing page creates awareness, provides education, aids in the decision making process and has a strong call to action that will move visitors quickly towards the conversion step. Make no mistake; if you want to be successful in creating an effective sales funnel, you're going to need to develop landing pages for the products that you are going to sell.

Once you've made the landing page, start directing traffic towards those pages through Facebook ads. Remember, you want to isolate the attention of your potential customers. By keeping your customers on Facebook the entire time, you risk them growing distracted. Don't use ads to redirect them to other spots on Facebook; use ads to get them to visit your landing page!

Principle Four: Monitor Performance

The sales funnel is not a one and done scenario. You don't just set one up and then watch as the dollar bills flow in. You must constantly be working to adjust the funnel to improve its performance. This requires close attention to how your customers are moving through the funnel.

How do we monitor customer activity? Through a series of different types of analytic software. Your Facebook pixel will provide Facebooks' analytics with a lot of information, data that you can sift through to determine the overall behavior of your site visitors. You'll be able to see how many are visiting, what they are clicking or interacting with and how many are actually converting. This data, when combined with the metrics provided by Facebook Ad campaigns, will give you a general idea of the performance of sales funnel as a whole. But that is not the only type of data that you want to be monitoring.

The second type of data you'll need to pay attention to is the bounce rate of the website itself. If a customer visits a single page on your website and then leaves afterward, that is known as a "bounce." In general, you want to have as low a bounce rate as possible. You will want to have your visitors look at multiple pages so that they can increase their awareness of your products.

You are using a website analytics platform, such as Google Analytics a great way to keep an eye on the bounce rate of your website. Google Analytics can monitor traffic from any source, report on where that traffic is coming from and can provide you with vital data, such as the bounce rate of your website, how long the average visit is, etc. These details are necessary for you to know. If you see that you have a high bounce rate, you can begin working to improve your website so that it draws the customer to click on more pages.

Another valuable tool in your monitoring toolkit is what is known as a heatmap. A heatmap is a type of software that monitors where people are clicking and moving their mouse around the most on a site. These clicks and actions will end up creating a map of cool, warm and hot areas on your website, giving you an impression of exactly what on your site is capturing their attention. This is important for understanding how consumers are educating themselves on your products. If certain areas are dead cold, you can revise them until they begin generating more interest from the traffic that you are generating.

Cart abandonment tools are necessary if you want to attempt to recapture the attention of those who placed something in their cart and then decided to exit. These tools detect when a cart has been abandoned, determines if you have the email of the person who left and if an email is on the register, will send a reminder about their cart being full. You can even customize these abandonment tools to send special discounts or offers that could motivate the abandoner to return and make the purchase.

These tools are necessary if you want to be able to fine-tune your sales funnel. All funnels start out one way: untested. Over time, you will be able to get a picture of how well your funnel is performing. Low performance means that you see very few conversions or worse, that conversions simply cost you too much. High performance means that you are able to generate a significant number of conversions while keeping costs low and stable.

Chapter 6: YouTube Essentials

Finding success on YouTube isn't an easy road; it takes a lot of work. However, if you are willing to put in the time, you can very well find tremendous success through YouTube, increasing your sales and even monetize your viewership through ad revenue. Let's take a look at some of the essential things that you need to know!

How YouTube Algorithms work in 2019

YouTube is more than just a place to host videos; it is also a search engine and a recommendation system. YouTube will look at a user's search and viewing history, then using advanced algorithms, will make suggestions to the viewer. As a content creator, these suggestions are vital to helping your content get discovered.

The key to increasing the chances of your channel and videos being suggested is to learn how to YouTube's algorithms make the decision. Once you have a handle of exactly how and why videos end up in the suggestion section, you can then tailor your content to increase the chances of discovery.

The algorithms themselves are designed to do one and only one thing: provide the most high quality and relevant content to consumers. For example, if a user is continually looking up tutorials on how to draw, YouTube will look for similar videos to the one that the user has watched. It will then rank these videos based on a certain number of factors, and if the videos are deemed relevant enough, they will be placed in the user's feed. So what factors do YouTube's algorithms look at?

Keywords:

Remember, YouTube is a part of Google, which is the king of the search engine. This means that YouTube pays the same level of attention when it comes to relevant keywords.

The right short and long-form keywords, organically used, can make all the difference when it comes to content discovery.

YouTube looks for keywords in your descriptions, your titles, your tags and even inside of your SRT files, which are transcriptions of your video. The more relevant the keywords that you have placed inside of your description, the better YouTube will be able to understand the video's relevance to your target audience.

Views:

YouTube rewards success. The more views that your video has, the better chance you have of being brought to new audiences. However, if a user is already following your videos, either through clicking the follow button or simply watches a lot of your content, YouTube will most likely put any brand new videos you post in their feed since it understands that the user is a fan of yours. However, this doesn't help when it comes to discovery. In order to have your video placed on new user's feeds, you will need to have enough views to signal to YouTube that your video is worth watching. YouTube wants to provide its viewers with good videos, and the biggest indicator of whether a video is good or not is a democratic process. People vote with their eyes, and YouTube pays attention to those votes.

It might not seem fair that those who get the most views will automatically increase their organic traffic due to these algorithms. But at the end of the day, YouTube wants to make money. They take a cut from ad revenue and the more views, the more money they make. So they have an incentive to take those who are proven to be successful and help them increase their success through recommendations.

Viewing Time:

Just like views are important, so is viewing time. YouTube can tell how long a user stays on a specific video and will use that data to rank that video. Low-quality videos are often abandoned quickly, usually once the viewer realizes that the video has either misled them or is just not worth the time. If a video has a high abandonment rate, YouTube will make sure not to include it in their recommendation areas. However, if videos have higher viewing times, usually going past the halfway mark, then it will show that there is a value within the video itself.

Content:

YouTube, recently, has begun to analyze more than merely the quality of content, but also the purpose of that content. Wishing to be more of a safe area, they have begun working to deplatform or demonetize content that they deem to be inappropriate. Certain political topics, conspiracy theories or hate speech can all be flagged by YouTube, and the platform could potentially be taken down. The best way to avoid all of this would be to learn their terms of service, what kind of content they deem to be appropriate and then to stay within the perimeter. As long as you aren't producing inflammatory videos or using hate speech, you should be safe.

Really, the three elements above are what defines what YouTube's algorithms are looking for. Things such as video length, which were a significant part of YouTube's algorithms in the past, have been downplayed. There is no current ideal video length since YouTube is focused more on viewing time and quality.

Proper Use of Titles, Description, and Thumbnails

Now that we have an understanding of how YouTube makes decisions for sharing content with users, you can begin working on creating good titles and descriptions. A good title and description is succinct, has the proper keywords for your target demographic and most importantly, is accurate to the video you are presenting.

While it is possible for larger YouTubers to get away with certain levels of dishonesty in descriptions or "clickbaity" titles, this is because they already have quite a large following. Their viewers will watch the videos they put out, regardless of the descriptions. However, as a smaller YouTuber, you don't have the same level of luxury.

You must be 100% honest about your videos. Don't use fake or gimmicky titles or thumbnails. If you do this, you may end up causing frustration in the viewer, who will then quickly abandon the video. This will hurt your numbers and more importantly, your viewing time, which puts you lower on the ranking system. Remember, those who rank lowest don't get their videos recommended at all!

A good description is quick and to the point. It gives the reader a chance to know what the video is about. While it is true that you can use descriptions as a valuable opportunity for placing keywords, you must be careful not to try and "stuff" your description with them. Keyword stuffing is the practice of simply writing out a long list of keywords, usually in an incoherent manner.

A good example of using keywords(in bold) in a YouTube description would be similar to this: “My **game review** of the stealth **action shooter Deus Ex**.” This is a good description because it is simple, coherent and includes several keywords that most people are going to be looking up. An example of keyword stuffing would like so: “My game review of the stealth action shooter Deus Ex. **Video games, game review, gaming, games, stealth games, action, Deus Ex, Square Enix, etc.**”

Keyword stuffing worked at one point, back in the early day of search algorithms and SEO. Now, engines have been designed to notice keyword stuffing and to ignore them. Why? To avoid manipulation, for the most part. If keyword stuffing worked effectively, then people could redirect anyone to their videos, even if the video didn’t have relevant content.

Try to focus on finding quality keywords that are relevant to both your audience and to the description of your video. There's no reason to try and game the system, as YouTube has grown much more aware of these attempts and will work to prevent them from working.

Thumbnails follow the same rules as creating titles. Make them clean, punchy and above all, avoid any kind of falsehoods. Don't include images that aren't actually in the video, as this is extremely misleading. Instead, try to create a compelling, clear graphic that lets readers tell what your video is about in less than a second. Good visual design, eye-catching graphics, and a good copy can work wonders in getting people to click on your video.

Chapter 7: Creating Quality YouTube Content

One of the more significant changes in the way YouTube recommends videos is that it is now a lot less focused on channels. At one time, having a prominent and popular channel meant that your channel would also be recommended more. However, as YouTube continues to grow in popularity, it now focusing on promoting videos themselves. While channels still have value to you as a content creator, the fact is, if you want to find real success on YouTube, you'll need to develop good, quality videos.

There is no secret formula to what makes for the perfect YouTube video. You can't just plug in a few elements and then watch something grow viral. However, there are principals and practices that you can incorporate into your videos that will increase the quality of your video, which increases the chances of getting committed viewers to watch your content. Let's take a look at some of these principles.

Principle One: The Viewers Matter Most

While there are many reasons to create YouTube videos, the fact remains that you are providing a service. Like any service, the customer is the most important part of the equation. You must keep your viewers in mind as you work on creating your videos. Ask yourself, will my viewers like this? Is this video honest? Is it enjoyable? What can I do to improve the viewing experience?

If you go into content creation with the mindset of focusing only on how you can make your own life better, either through monetization or going viral, you will end up setting yourself up for failure. Content creation is a service based on the principals of exchange. A viewer trades their attention and time in exchange for something that perceives to be valuable for them. If they don't perceive value, they won't engage.

Therefore, it is of the utmost importance that you put your viewers first when making content creation decisions. Try to determine what viewers in your niche are looking for, what they would find valuable and then craft that content. By giving them what they want, you are increasing the chances of them engaging with your content. By creating what you want to create and paying no mind to consumer demands or interests, you are seriously limiting your ability to generate views.

Principle Two: Differentiate Yourself

It can be easy to look at YouTubers who have achieved tremendous success and think that imitation is the best way to find the same success. And while there is something to be said about learning from those who have already made it to the top, directly copying others is not the way to go. Yet, whenever a new and successful format or YouTuber rises, there are often thousands upon thousands of copycats trying to imitate that format. Most of these videos only get a few hits. Why? Usually, it's for one of two reasons.

The first reason is that most of these copycat videos aren't of any decent quality. They are poorly made, weakly written and don't carry any of the value that the most popular video in that format has. This means that not only is it a copycat, it's also a more inferior version of the original. Why would anyone bother to watch a poorly made knock-off when they could just watch the original?

The second reason is brand loyalty. YouTubers often do more than simply create videos; they create brands. These are individual styles that they apply to their own videos that set them apart from the competition. Whether it's a performance type of brands, such as snarkiness or intelligent analysis, or a visual brand, such as clear cut visuals and sharp lettering, these brands differentiate the YouTuber from the pack of competitors.

Part of creating good content is differentiating yourself from the competition. If you can be original in your video format and that format is enjoyable, you have a step ahead, since you're not copying anyone else. However, there are formats that are time tested and proven to generate interest from viewers. For example, videos featuring a Top 10 collection of facts pertaining to a specific niche is extremely popular. YouTubers across the board can create these Top 10 videos about all sorts of topics, usually in their chosen niche. Since there are virtually unlimited subjects to talk about, anyone can make a Top 10 video.

What will differentiate you from the competition when creating a video based on an accessible format is a combination of quality and style. Quality speaks for itself. If you can create a crisp, fast and good looking video, you will automatically put yourself a large step above the competition. The vast majority of videos on YouTube aren't very good in terms of quality, so by putting in the required time and effort to make a nice looking and sounding video, you'll be doing yourself a huge favor.

The second way to differentiate yourself is through style. Every big YouTuber has a specific style, a method of presentation that they use to put a spin on the content they are sharing. Even those YouTubers who talk about things like the news have their own methods of delivery, which distinguishes them from others out there.

Creating your own style takes time. But it is something that you'll need to consider as you begin branching out into the world of content creation. The style is really up to how you want to present your material. Do you want to have some kind of persona? Is there some common thread that runs throughout all of your videos? Will each video have the same kind of narration and if so, what does the narrator sound like? There are literally thousands of questions that you can ask yourself when it comes to creating your own style.

Don't worry too much about getting your style nailed down right away. Over time, you will continue to develop that style until finally, you are able to create a type of content brand consistently. Until you reach the point of having a fully developed style, just be thinking about how you present your content and how to make your presentation unique. Remember, the more you can differentiate yourself from the competition, the better chance you have of developing a following.

Principle Three: Production Quality First

When we say high-quality content, we're actually referring to two separate qualities. The first is production quality and the second is content quality. If you want to be successful, you'll need to work on developing in both areas. However, when it comes to learning how to create quality videos, the first thing that you'll want to focus on developing is production quality.

Production quality refers to the design of the actual video itself. All aspects of production quality can either hinder or help your video. Low production quality can quickly turn someone off to a video, while high production quality can increase the number of times a video is rewatched.

Now, this discussion of production quality is all about creating the bare minimum for good production. Most likely, you aren't going to have unlimited resources when it comes to creating videos, especially if you're just getting started. While it is possible to have excellent production quality by spending a fortune on it, a high budget isn't necessary to create good production quality. Instead, in order to have good production quality, you just need to focus on three areas: sound, recording, and editing.

Sound:

Audio is one of the most important elements of production quality. If viewers cannot easily hear the presentation, if there is some kind of loud buzzing the background, or noise that interrupts the flow of the performance, a viewer will quickly grow irritated. Fortunately, creating good audio isn't terribly hard to do. All you need is to make sure that you have a decent quality microphone that is able to record without picking up background noise. We'll be covering hardware for YouTubers in a later chapter, where we'll have recommendations for microphones for any budget.

Video:

The video is also another necessary component of production quality. After all, people are watching YouTube for the videos. Proper recording methods, ensuring that the video isn't shaky, blurry or filmed from a strange angle will go a long way in making your videos enjoyable. While there can be an incredibly high price point that comes with getting recording equipment, for the most part, you can make do with the cheaper options, such as using your phone.

Part of what helps in recording good video productions is lighting. If you're going to be recording yourself, or someone else talking, then a lighting kit would most likely be necessary. A lighting kit contains everything necessary to illuminate yourself properly, so that you look great on the camera and that there is no glare, no reflections or weirdness that can come from using improper lighting.

Editing:

While audio and recording combined are what creates the raw product, you'll need to be skilled at editing if you want to make these videos polished and ready for uploading. Editing is a technical skill that requires special software to use. Good editing allows for you to fix errors in recording, clean up the audio so that it's crisp and most importantly, add text and graphics to your videos.

Learning how to edit well is time-consuming, but is one of the necessary elements of creating videos with excellent production quality. If you don't want to learn how to edit, you'll have to find a professional editor to do the work for you.

These three areas combined, sound, video, and editing are where you will want to focus on perfecting first. Now, while there is always room for improvement, you will want to get your productions to a point where for the most part, they are free from errors. This comes with time and practice. There will be a lot of things to learn as you go about your quest of creating quality videos, but at the beginning, you'll want to focus on creating the highest quality videos that you can with the resources that you have. Once you have this part figured out, you'll be able to apply those principles to any video that you choose. Sure it might be time-consuming at first, but it is well worth it.

Principle Four: Stay In Your Niche

When you're starting out, you may be tempted to try and bring in as much traffic as you can to your videos by creating content that would appeal to just about everyone. However, the goal isn't simply to get people to view your one video, but rather to view multiple videos on your channel and ultimately follow you. Rather than try to create videos that appeal to everyone, focus on targeting a specific niche. There is just too much content on YouTube to gain a wide appeal, at least in the beginning.

Instead, focus on creating content for your niche exclusively. Each time you go to make a video, analyze what your target demographic is looking for and then produce videos to meet that niche's need. The more videos that appeal to a specific niche, the better chance you have of viewers going from one of your video to another. However, if you have a bunch of videos that are unrelated to each other, then viewers most likely won't check out the others.

Principle Five: Just Get To The Content

One tremendous frustration that most viewers experience is when they click on a video but have to wait a solid 3 or 4 minutes to get to the actual content. Videos that offer to solve problems, but have 5 straight minutes to wait because of someone talking about how excited they are about the channel or telling some news will often be abandoned quickly.

People are busy. Every time that someone clicks on your video, they could be watching a different video, and they are keenly aware of that fact. If you are promising some kind of content for them, such as a how-to, troubleshooting or news about something, but then take forever to actually get to the subject, you are not doing any favors to your viewers. New viewers will probably just click away. And those who have to jump ahead to get to the actual content will just be irritated.

So really, when it comes to creating the format of your video just get to the relevant and important content as soon as possible. Patience is a rare virtue online, and you'll want to capture your viewer's attention as quickly as possible. Resist the urge to plug other videos or your channel until after you've given the valuable information. Viewers will be grateful and will most likely be willing to engage with other content.

Principle Six: Create Long-Term Content Strategies

Once you have the attention of a viewer, you'll need to give them an incentive to subscribe to your channel. The best incentive is to have a long term content strategy, creating videos in a series and clearly labeling them. If someone sees that a video has been branded part 1 and part 2 isn't out yet, they may subscribe in the hopes of being alerted when part 2 releases.

You should always be working to create content as part of a series. This will help you get an idea of what type of content you should be making next, as well as capture the attention of interested viewers. If someone likes the first video in a series, they will most likely watch the second, third and so on. This will significantly increase your viewing times, which in turn assists in boosting your rankings on YouTube.

Chapter 8: Growing Your YouTube Channel

Once you've put in the time and energy to create a few videos, you'll probably be itching to grow as quickly as possible. The good news is that you can absolutely grow your YouTube channel in just a few short months. However, this takes a lot of focus and discipline, especially if you want to grow as quickly as possible. Let's take a look at a few different ways that you can quickly grow your YouTube channel.

Growth Tip 1: Integrate a Subscribe button in your videos

If you want to grow, you're going to need subscribers who will watch your videos as you create them. While YouTube does have a subscribe button located a few inches down, some viewers will be watching your video on a fullscreen mode. By integrating a subscribe button into the actual video itself, all the viewer has to do is click or tap on the link inside of the video, which will then subscribe to them.

Growth Tip 2: Create links to other videos inside your video

When a user has finished watching your video, you will want to try and get them to see some of your other work, especially if they are new to your channel. A great way to do this would be to create a little boxed preview of your other videos at the end of each video. These previews can be clicked which will then take the viewer straight to the other video. This is a great way to refer users to other videos of yours.

Growth Tip 3: Use Paid Advertising

One of the fastest ways to kickstart your YouTube growth would be to simply use paid advertising to link your target demographic to your videos. By using Facebook Ads or Google Ads, you can put your videos in front of people who would be interested enough to watch them.

And if they watch your videos, they have a chance of converting and becoming followers.

The downside to paid advertising is that it'll cost you money. But, if you're planning on growing your channel so that you can monetize, it might be worth the investment. We'll discuss monetization in the next chapter. Just know that using a paid advertising engine is a great way to boost your channel growth in the short term.

Growth Tip 4: Cross Promote on Other Social Media Platforms

While YouTube is great for hosting content, it's not terribly good for sharing content. While they do have some limited social media functions, the fact is that other platforms such as Facebook or Twitter are better suited for sharing content. If you want to be able to share your content with others quickly and make it so that others can quickly share your content with their friends, you should cross-promote on your chosen social media platforms.

For example, after you upload a video on YouTube, you'll want to create a separate post on Facebook or your other preferred social media platforms. Include the link so that others can quickly see it and if they like the content, they can share it.

While this is an important part of doing your due diligence, you must remember that most social media platforms don't want to give companies a bunch of free advertising. They've developed algorithms to prevent users from spamming videos and other content over and over again, often making it harder for these videos to reach others organically.

In order to combat this, try limiting your posting to only a few times a week. Don't overpost and don't only post about your own content. Instead, try to take a balanced approach, sharing relevant content and talking about things other than your own channel. This will help grow your social media network as well as show others that you care about more than just your own success.

Growth Tip 5: Make friends with other YouTubers

Just because you are in competition with other YouTubers for views doesn't mean that you can't be friends. There are enough viewers out there to go around, so don't think of other YouTubers in your niche as enemies. Instead, look at them as potential allies. A good relationship with another YouTuber can be mutually beneficial. By mentioning each other on your channels, referring to each other's content and promoting one another, you are both increase your chances of gaining new viewers.

There are a lot of benefits from making friends with other channels. One of the most significant benefits is that you can potentially guest star on their videos, or you can ask them to guest star on one of yours. This has a tremendous benefit because either way, it will direct an already established viewership towards your channel. Likewise, your own viewership will also be directed towards their channel.

What's the best strategy for making friends? In general, you'll want to be cordial, reach out to them and ask if they're interested in collaborating on a project. Don't, however, try to aim too high, especially if you're brand new. Going after a YouTuber who has an established 15 million subscribers while you only have a few hundred will most likely not yield you any results. Try instead to aim for the middle, look for YouTubers who have grown quite a bit, but aren't so high that they'd basically be doing you a favor by working with you.

Remember, the best chance of building a relationship with another YouTuber is to offer them some kind of value. Value is in the quality of your content, the number of followers that you have or the willingness that you have to promote them. Most YouTubers aren't looking to work with someone who is purely interested in simply exploiting them so that they can gain more views. Instead, they are looking for a mutual relationship or even a real friendship, which will provide both parties a benefit.

Growth Tip 6: Have a Frequent Upload Schedule

The more videos that you have, the more a person will watch, especially if they really like the content you're creating. And, as we've talked about in terms of YouTube's algorithm, the longer watch time you have, the better chances your videos will show up in people's recommended feed. Therefore, it is of the utmost importance for you to have a frequent upload schedule, so you can create a backlog for viewers to enjoy.

On top of creating a larger and larger backlog, the more you upload, the more subscribers will see that you are an active YouTuber. They may even get into the habit of watching videos that you make almost as soon as you upload them, merely because they expect you to upload quite frequently and are looking forward to the new videos.

What's the ideal upload ratio? In general, if you can get at least one video out a week, you're doing pretty well and taking longer than a week may cause interest to diminish in your channel. It is important to note that while you want to have a regular, frequent content update, you don't want to release unpolished or unfinished videos. Definitely, don't try and pick quantity over quality.

A good practice is to create a few videos ahead of time, then release them on a weekly basis. This will give you a cushion, so you don't have to worry about falling behind on your production, and it will show viewers that you are quite active. Then, as you create new videos, you simply add them to the pile and release them as needed. Having a backlog to release will help prevent you from needing to rush a job out.

Growth Tip 7: Create Playlists

A playlist is a collection of YouTube videos that have been assembled together by a creator. Then, when one video ends, the playlist automatically plays the next video on that list. Once you have created a series of videos, you can create a better viewer experience by creating a playlist of that series. Then, all a viewer has to do is click on the playlist and it will automatically take them through all of the content you've put in that list.

Why do this? Simply enough, it lessens the amount of input needed from the viewer. Since they don't have to interact with clicking the next video, they won't be potentially distracted by something else. There are many times where a viewer goes to click on the next video, but something else in their feed pulls them away.

Growth Tip 8: Don't Buy Views

As you are working to grow your channel and your views, you may end up coming across certain websites that promise to provide you with thousands of views in exchange for a small fee. Some companies will even add subscribers to the list, all you have to do is swipe your credit card, and then online fame can be yours! Except for the fact that this majorly violates YouTube's terms of service.

YouTube wants to sell ads, and in order to sell those ads properly, views need to be from real people, not computers. When you purchase views from these websites, they use bots to fulfill those requirements. If YouTube takes notice that you have an unusually high number of bots visiting your videos, they will demonetize your video. It's possible that your account could even be suspended.

On top of those risks, there is the fact that fake traffic and subscribers aren't real growth at all. Sure, you can spend a few hundred to boost your channel up to a high number, but you aren't actually going to profit from those views. You want real people to be watching your videos. Fake numbers do nothing other than draining your bank account and throws off your ability to read metrics.

These view peddlers are really nothing more than complicated fraudsters, happy to take your money and promise you all sorts of great results. The truth is, hard work and determination will be the thing that grows your channel. And if you're going to spend money on getting views, you might as well do it the honest way by using Facebook or Google Ads. At least those services won't get your account banned.

Growth Tip 9: Engage with Commenters

The YouTube comments section has unfortunately developed a reputation for being a terrible cesspool, full of trolls and cretins who wish to cause pain and suffering to others. This reputation has been earned by the unfortunate fact that anonymity often allows people to act unfiltered. Since they won't have to suffer from the consequences of their actions, they can behave; however, they wish online. Oftentimes this translates into hurtful words and cruelty.

However, just because there are commenters out there who wish to naysay, troll and otherwise cause harm to others doesn't mean that you should ignore the comments. If you wish to grow your channel, you'll need to have a personal relationship with your viewers. You should be willing to go through the comments, wading through the trash in order to find the gems.

Answering questions, thanking people for feedback and sharing thoughts is a great way to connect to followers. This will, in turn, create a better sense of relationship and will motivate the follower to continue watching your shows.

Yet, handling comments is a tricky business. You need to be extremely careful in how you approach things such as trolling and criticism. The most important thing to learn is how to distinguish between someone who's just being a troll and someone who has legitimate criticism. For example, if a person were to comment “The audio is just unbearably bad,” we can recognize that this is a legitimate criticism. If a person were to say “this video sucks,” this most likely isn’t a legitimate attempt to give feedback, but rather a troll just trying to get a rise out of you.

Why should you learn the difference between the two? Because legitimate criticism should be responded to, but trolls should be ignored. If your viewers have legitimate complaints, you should listen to them and adapt to them, apologize if necessary. However, if a troll is just trying to stir up trouble, you should ignore them entirely.

Some people make the mistake of engaging with trolls, in an attempt to one-up them. The problem here is that oftentimes a troll simply enjoys the process of causing trouble and getting a response will only encourage them. Worse yet, if they get the better of you, they may lure you into saying something foolish that you will come to regret later. There is just no reason to engage with a troll. Don't respond to it; don't play into their trap. Simply ignore them and move on.

Chapter 9: A Guide to Collaboration

As we mentioned in the previous chapter, one of the best ways to expand your channel is to focus on collaborating with other YouTubers. We've outlined the philosophy of providing value, and the mutual relationship earlier, so we won't cover that here. Rather, we want to provide you with a step by step framework on how to properly collaborate with other YouTubers.

Step One: Establish Your Channel

The first step is to really make sure that your channel is well established. This doesn't mean that you have to have a ton of viewers, or that you need to be wildly successful, but you should have everything in order before you start reaching out to others. Have a decent backlog of videos, enough so that a YouTuber examining your channel will see that you are somewhat serious about what you are doing. Make sure that the descriptions are well written, the thumbnails are clean and attractive and that everything about your channel is presentable.

Step Two: Create a shortlist

Once you have your channel established and presentable, it's time for you to go out and start looking for YouTubers whom you could possibly collaborate with. The first thing to keep in mind when creating your shortlist is that you only want to have YouTubers who are in relevant spaces to your niche. For example, if you're running a gaming channel, you will want to look for YouTubers in that same field. Picking YouTubers outside of your target demographic is a waste of time.

The second thing to pay attention to is the size of the channel and their viewership. In general, you want to aim for the middle, find YouTubers who aren't so big that your request would get lost in the tidal wave of emails they receive on a daily basis. Rather than trying to chase after a single person, spread out your interests and look for viewers who garner tens of thousands of views, or even hundreds of thousands.

Once you've located the more successful YouTubers, take note of what type of content they produce, their personalities and their style. Ask yourself if you two would get along. Would you be able to work with this person professionally? Do you actually like their style and videos? If you don't genuinely enjoy their work, then you are most likely going to struggle in being sincere and authentic with them. No one wants to work with a crass opportunist who feigns interest, only to further their own goals.

With all of that data, you should be able to put together a list of YouTubers that you will want to collaborate with. Try to get at least 4 or 5 names on that list, so that you can work on them one at a time, to see who would be interested.

Step Three: Connect to the YouTuber

Reaching out is a vital step when it comes to collaboration. And of course, it can be the most uncomfortable step as well, especially if you aren't someone who likes to self-promote. However, it is one of the necessary evils. Fortunately, all you need is for one of your efforts to succeed, and then you'll be able to work on developing content together and growing your channel!

The first impression is important. Make sure that you are familiar with the potential collaborator's work, enough so that you can reference it. This will do well in showing the collaborator that you are willing to put in the research and also that you care enough about their work to actually watch it.

When you're ready to reach out, you will want to figure out a way to contact them. Unless they have a website or some kind of email readily available, you'll want to try and go through social media. Don't just post in the YouTube comments about a collaboration, rather add them on their preferred social media and then send them a private message.

The message should be succinct, straightforward and clearly outlines your intentions. You'll want to introduce yourself first, talk briefly about your channel, what it's about and what type of content you host. Don't brag or try to puff yourself up; just let them know who you are.

After you introduce yourself, get straight to the point of the email. Let them know that you are interested in a collaboration, outline a bit of what you have in mind and then ask them if they would be interested in working with you. Be cordial and polite, don't make promises and don't try to flatter them too much.

The email you send should be rather short. Try to keep it under a few hundred words. If they are interested, they'll reply, and then you'll have more time to talk. But an unsolicited wall of text will most likely not be met with enthusiasm by the potential collaborator.

It's also important that you only reach out to one collaborator at a time. The last thing that you want to deal with is four potential collaborators whom all say yes at the exact same time. While that may be a good problem to have, it will work out better if you take the slower approach, that way you don't alienate any potential collaborator down the road. If your answer is yes, but you only have the time or resources to work with one, you've essentially snubbed the other three.

Step Four: Deal with the response

Hopefully, you'll receive a response from the potential collaborator. If the response is a no, then don't worry about it. You may feel disappointed, or a bit rejected, but there are dozens of reasons why a Youtuber would say no. Sure, it doesn't feel right to hear a no, but there are plenty of other YouTubers out there. Don't let that discourage you and keep looking for people to work with.

Silence can also be a problem. Ideally, you should get a response within a week or two, but if you find yourself waiting past that, you should most likely move on. Either the YouTuber didn't bother to reply, lost track of your email or simply didn't have the time to open it and read.

If you receive a yes from the collaborator, then that's great news! You can then begin working out the details of creating a collaboration project together. You can work on not only creating a video together but also fostering an active and healthy relationship with the YouTuber.

Step Five: Build a Network

Once you have accomplished your first collaboration effort, you should work to promote it as much as you can. Keep your new friend in mind when it comes to making recommendations, be willing to send traffic to them and stay in the loop with them. Over time, you can work to find more people to collaborate with and soon, you'll have built your very own network!

Chapter 10: Monetizing YouTube

YouTube can be a very lucrative platform, as long as you know how to do it right. Most of the time, when a person thinks about financial success on YouTube, they simply think of YouTube's revenue sharing program. However, selling ads on YouTube is one of four ways that you can monetize your YouTube channel. Let's take a look at all four.

Monetization Method One: YouTube Ads

It's no secret that YouTube wants to sell ad space to advertisers. They share a percentage of the ad space that they sell with content creators who are part of the revenue sharing model. As long as people are watching and clicking on ads, a creator can get paid.

How much money the creator makes is based on a number of things. The first and most obvious is the number of views that a video has.

The more views, the more times an ad is seen. And the more an ad is seen, the more advertisers pay YouTube. YouTube then pays a percentage out to the content creator.

However, while ad revenue is an important part of monetization on YouTube, the fact is that in order to make a significant amount of money, you'd need to reach millions of viewers per video. This means making money off of YouTube's ad program alone isn't as easy as it sounds. You won't be making anything serious until after you have quite a dedicated following of viewers.

Don't let this discourage you, however. YouTube is a vast company, and billions of videos are watched on a daily basis. You absolutely can reach millions of views per video. Getting it isn't easy; it takes time and effort. But once you finally reach that point, you will find that you'll be able to make a few thousand per video easily.

The good news is that even if you aren't able to reach those numbers right away, ads are only one way to make money on YouTube. There are quite a few other methods, so don't worry if you aren't raking in cash from ad revenue just yet. There are other ways to monetize your content.

Monetization Method Two: Patreon

As a content creator, you have a unique connection and relationship with your viewers. You are able to address them directly, build relationships and create the content that keeps them coming back for more and more. With websites like Patreon, you can actually gain their direct financial support on a monthly basis.

Patreon allows users to sign up and support content creators, committing a certain amount of money per month. In exchange, you as the content creator can give them access to exclusive content that can't be found anywhere else. For example, you can have exclusive videos that only people who pledge $5 a month or more can access.

This allows you to gain support from fans who love your content and want to help you create more through a financial contribution. In exchange, they get special stuff that non-patrons cannot have access to. It's a win-win situation. And the best part is that patrons pay out monthly, which means as long as you have people who pledge to pay, you'll be turning a profit each month.

There really aren't any downsides to using a support system like Patreon. Sure, some followers might not like the idea that you are offering exclusive content in exchange for pay, but then again, you're offering a free service. If they aren't happy with you getting paid for some of your work, then they most likely would never agree to financially support you anyway.

The best way to monetize a patron is to create one with multiple tiers, ranging from $1-5 a month. Each tier should grant access to certain types of exclusive content. You'll want to make sure that your content is valuable enough to motivate viewers to subscribe. And you'll also want to make sure that your content is being released monthly, as a way to retain your subscribers from month to month.

Once you've created your Patreon, be sure to include a link to it on your YouTube channel and promote it from time to time on some of your videos. Make sure to focus most on what type of content is available, so that users will be excited to sign up.

Monetization Method Three: Sponsorship

As YouTubers are becoming more and more influential, companies are beginning to see the real financial value of working with YouTubers. By offering to sponsor channels, these companies are often able to generate more brand awareness and promote their products. And the best part about sponsorship is that you don't have to be some giant channel to be able to secure it. All you really need is to display that you have the right demographic for your sponsors.

There are two ways to gain company sponsorships with YouTube. The first is to use YouTube's FameBit program. FameBit is a hub that connects YouTubers with sponsors. This allows you to simply apply to the program, then browse from a list of available sponsors. Then, you just need to send in an application and see if they'd be interested in sponsoring your content. If they are, they'll pay you a set amount, from which YouTube will take a small cut.

The second way to gain sponsorship is to go outside of YouTube and find a company or program that is willing to connect content creators with sponsors. You'll have to go through an application process and convince them why your channel is worth sponsoring, but if you pull it off, you'll be able to earn some money from a corporate sponsor.

Sponsorship isn't a guaranteed way to make money. You'll have to be able to demonstrate what makes you worth investing in; you'll most likely need a decent amount of viewership as well as a strong brand identity. However, if things are going well with your channel and you feel confident, there's no reason not to try and make some money by applying for sponsorships.

Monetization Method Four: Selling Products

While you can't sell anything directly through YouTube, you can direct your viewers to your online store. If you're looking to monetize your efforts, selling merchandise, specialty items and other products are the way to go.

When viewers experience a connection with a YouTuber, they are more willing to trust that YouTuber's recommendations. On top of that, those who especially like the content creator will often want to show their appreciation by purchasing merchandise related to the YouTuber themselves. You can capitalize on this by creating an online store and selling products related to your channel.

Of course, not everyone has the capacity to print merchandise on their own. It can be extremely costly to get your own merchandise business going, as you'll need to absorb the cost of printing t-shirts, bumper stickers, and window decals, right? Well, not exactly! Thanks to the power of on-demand printing websites like Redbubble, you can sell your own merchandise without having to pay anything upfront.

These services provide you with everything you need to create your own merchandise. All you need is the artwork to upload to their systems; then from then on, they will offer t-shirts, mugs, hats and all sorts of other products to your customers. When a customer purchases the item, a third party puts your art on the product and then ships it out to the customer. You get paid a margin, Redbubble takes their cut, and the customer gets merchandise with your branding on it.

The value of a service like this is that you don't have to spend any capital on merchandise. You don't have to deal with shipping and handling, bulk orders, or any of those other headaches. Rather, you just let Redbubble handle all of those details. The only thing you need to worry about is getting paid.

However, this is a few drawbacks to these services. The first is that you aren't getting too large of a commission. Redbubble will be taking the bulk of the profits as they are the ones who are doing all of the heavy liftings. This means in order to make serious money off of your merchandise; you're going to have to move a lot of product in volume. Still, if you're just starting out, you're saving a fortune from having to invest in your own merchandise.

The second drawback is the fact that you don't have a direct hand in quality control. The good news is that most of these print on demand websites like Redbubble are dedicated to sourcing from quality manufacturers, but there can be slip ups on occasion. And if that's the case, you might end up having to smooth things over with a frustrated customer.

Can a Business Profit From Using YouTube?

One question you might be asking if you're not interested in pursuing YouTube on a career level is whether it is profitable or not for you to use YouTube anyway. The answer is a resounding yes! Even if you aren't planning on becoming a serious content creator who wants to make revenue from selling ad space, you should still be willing to use YouTube.

Why? Because as a business there are certain types of content that you can produce that will help your customers when moving through your sales funnel. Let's take a look at some of the different types of videos that you can produce for your customers.

Tutorials:

If the products that you are selling have a specific function that might be complicated or difficult to use, you might want to consider investing some time in creating a tutorial. This will help your customers who have already made their purchases in solving simple problems. Better yet, you can even work to create tutorials that aren't directly related to your product, but rather are related to the niche you are serving. Then, as a consumer is looking to you for guidance and assistance on specific problems, they will be exposed to your brand. Over time, this exposure might end up netting you their business!

Advertisements:

If you want to promote your products through YouTube's ad system, then you're going to need your own videos. Creating advertisements for your own products is a great idea for multiple reasons. The first is that the distribution of those videos can be absolutely free. Rather than use YouTube's ad system, you could simply create your own video, then upload it onto your own website. Then, interested users can watch ads for your products as they explore around your website.

This will aid them fundamentally during the education phase and more importantly, doesn't cost you a dime. Since YouTube is the host and they absorb the cost of hosting, all you need to do is embed the link onto your page and let the views roll in.

Second, if you do decide to make an ad run, product advertisements can be great for generating brand awareness. A short video that catches the interest and eye of those in your target demographic can go a long way in bringing in new sales.

Product Demonstrations:

This is another excellent option for aiding a customer during the education phase. A product demonstration done by the creators will help demonstrate the value of the product. More importantly, it will also show the product in action, answering some of the questions that your viewers might have. Having a large backlog of product demonstrations for all of the relevant products in your inventory can boost sales over time.

Remember, the more information that you are able to provide a customer, the more educated they will be to make a purchasing decision. And, if your product demonstrations are well made, high energy and exciting, you can even motivate viewers to make the purchase as soon as quickly, which pushes them to the end step of the funnel.

Chapter 11: Equipment for YouTube

If you want to be a successful YouTuber, then you're going to need the right kind of gear to get the job done. The good news is that regardless of your budget, you have plenty of options to choose from. We're going to cover three budgets here, low, mid range and high end and show all the gear we recommend for each price range.

Video:

You can't have a YouTube video without the ability to record. So let's look at which cameras work best for any budget.

Low Budget Options:

Your Phone:

If you own a phone that's been produced in the last few years, especially an iPhone, you're actually all set for recording. While it might not have a lot of the features that an actual video camera has, a phone can record quality videos. If you're just doing a vlog, then you might want to save some money by simply using what you already have.

YI 4K Action and Sports Camera, 4K/30fps Video 12MP Raw Image with EIS, Live Stream, Voice Control:

Price: 104.65

The YI 4k Action and Sports Camera is excellent for recording just about anything. It's cost-effective, records in 4K and has a battery life of about 120 minutes. On top of that, there is wifi which allows for you to upload videos quickly and the device itself has been outfitted with impact resistant Gorilla Glass. If you're looking for a camera to record the action and sports-related activity, then you can't go wrong with the YI 4K.

Canon PowerShot ELPH 360 Digital Camera

Price: 179.000

The Canon PowerShot ELPH is a traditional digital camera, but with recording capabilities. It has image stabilization, which is extremely valuable, as well as the ability to film in low-light conditions. It's easy to use, simple to operate and is a Canon, which is one of the better camera brands out there. Most importantly, it's compact. If you don't want to have to lug around a bunch of equipment, the Canon PowerShot ELPH 360 is the right choice for you.

Sony Handycam CX405 Flash Memory Camcorder:

Price: 179.99

The Sony Handycam CX405 is a camcorder that is lightweight, simple to use and is excellent for beginners. It's suitable for recording simple events, although the battery life leaves a bit to be desired, as it lasts only three to four hours of recording time. However, it is on the cheap end for a video camera and will record in great quality.

Canon VIXIA HF R800

Price: 195.99

The Canon VIXIA HF R800 is on the higher end of low budget choices, but it is seriously worth it. Able to record in 60 fps, with image stabilization, if you're looking for a good camcorder that can record just about anything, this is the one for you. The only caveat is that you need to have good lighting, as the camera doesn't work as well in low-lighting situations. Other than that, this camera comes highly recommended for any YouTuber who is looking to make high-quality recordings.

Mid-Range Budget:

Nikon COOLPIX B500

Price: 256.95

The Nikon COOLPIX B500 is a great camera that contains a bevy of useful features. First off, it has great video quality, recording in both 1080p and 30 fps. On top of that, it is vibration resistant, so if you're going to be recording on the go, you'll have the ability to ignore bumps, thumps and other disturbances. Overall, it's a great mid-level camera.

Panasonic LUMIX FZ80

Price: 297.00

The Panasonic LUMIX FZ80 is a point and shoot digital camera, with recording capabilities. It can record in 4K with full HD capabilities, making for great, high-quality recordings. With a strong low-light function, the Panasonic LUMIX FZ80 is perfect for those who are looking for a right blend of photography and recording options.

Sony DSCHX80/B

Price: 318.00

The Sony DSCHX80/B is considered to be one of the best models for recording YouTube videos. It's incredibly portable, easy to use and has a manual mode, which makes for better recording options. With image stabilization, wifi and the ability to record in 60fps, this is one of the highest quality mid-range point and shoot cameras on the market. It's perfect for making videos and has plenty of options for customizing your recording experience.

High-End Budgets:

Canon PowerShot G7 X Mark II

Price: 649.00

The Canon PowerShot G7 Mark II is a high-end camera that will provide a professional recording experience. Able to capture full HD videos, the G7 Mark II is compact, easy to use and has been used by many other professional YouTubers such as PewDiePie. The flip screen makes it easy to use for recording on all angles, and the quality is very high. If you're looking for a higher end camera to start out with, the Canon PowerShot is a great choice.

Nikon D7200

Price: 696.95

The Nikon D7200 has a lot of great features, but the one that sets it apart from others is it's 51 point autofocus system. The camera can quickly focus, detecting new objects quickly and adjusting accordingly. If you're looking for a camera that can record high-quality 1080p videos at 60fps, then you might want to consider the D7200. It works well in low-light conditions, thanks to its focus system, has a good battery life of up to 6 hours of recording time and has built-in wireless capabilities.

Streaming Cameras:

If you're a streamer, then you're going to want a camera that is able to capture your face and reactions with high quality. While the above cameras are generally for recording, you'll want to choose a specialty camera designed to provide a flawless, lagless stream.

Logitech C922x Pro:

Price: 72.99

The Logitech C922x Pro is a great webcam that has excellent video quality, able to record up to 60 FPS at 720p, as well as 30 FPS at 1080p. It has a built-in lighting correction system, able to recognize when the stream is in low light and can improve visibility. In addition to these features, it also has a background replacement feature. So if you're live streaming and don't want your viewers to see what's going on behind you, you can put in a custom background behind you. While there are other webcams on the market, this is one is friendliest to those who want to live to stream their gaming, especially with the incorporation of that background replacement technology.

Audio Equipment:

While video equipment is an absolute necessity for creating YouTube videos, audio equipment is actually more important in a sense. Poor video can mostly be fixed by improving your filming, changing lighting, fixing angles, etc. However, there is no technique that can fix bad a lousy microphone. If you have to make a choice between an okay camera and a good microphone or a good camera and an okay microphone, take the good mic every time.

It's also important to note that while just about every camera has a built-in microphone, you're most likely not going to want to use those. They tend to be poor quality compared to an actual microphone. Let's look at low, medium and high budget microphones.

Low Budget Microphones:

Blue Snowball:

Price: 47.98

The Blue Snowball is compact, small and easy to operate. It has great audio capture and is dirt cheap. If you don't have much of a budget, we'd recommend going with the Snowball.

Blue Yeti:

Price: 129.00

The Blue Yeti is a condenser mic that has a host of excellent features. It has a built-in mute button and an omnidirectional recording pattern, meaning that you can use it to capture audio 360 degrees. There's a duo mode on the mic as well, so if you're interviewing, you can both share the same mic.

If you're a streamer or a YouTuber who doesn't need to leave the house when recording, then the Blue Yeti comes highly recommended. It provides crisp, and clean audio quality has a built-in condenser which makes for better noise reduction and uses a USB connector.

Medium Budget Microphones:

Rode NT-USB

Price: 169.00

The Rode NT-USB is similar to the Blue Yeti in that it is a cardioid mic that uses a USB cable instead of an auxiliary cable. With a built-in pop-shield and a tripod, this microphone captures clear quality audio with ease.

High Budget Microphones:

Rode VideoMic Pro Shotgun Microphone:

Price: 259.00

If you're going to be recording with a video camera on the go, you're most likely going to need audio equipment to go with it. The Rode VideoMic Pro is a shotgun microphone that attaches to your camera, allowing for you to capture sound perfectly while recording at the same time.

Pop-Filters:

While there can be an endless list of accessories to purchase for all of your gear, be it audio or video, we did feel that it is worth mentioning that you will most likely want to get a pop-filter for your microphone. A pop filter is a film of cloth that helps prevent puffs of air from striking the microphone. Usually, these pops come from saying letters with hard stops, such as p. The puff of air hits the mic, causing distortion which later has to be removed during editing.

A good pop-filter will keep those hard sounds out, reducing the amount of work that you'll have to do in the editing process. They aren't terribly expensive. You can get a good one for about ten or fifteen dollars. They aren't absolutely necessary to the recording process, but they do provide a lot of value for the price.

Editing Software:

Once you've actually recorded the videos, you're going to need to begin the process of editing. Editing software comes in all different shapes and sizes. Let's take a look at some of the most popular editing software on the market.

Low Budget Software:

Hitfilm Express:

Price: Free

OS: Windows

Hitfilm Express is a great video editing program for beginners. It's absolutely free to use, making it perfect for the YouTuber who is just starting out and doesn't have that high of a budget.

iMovie:

Price: Free

OS: Mac

iMovie is Apple's video editing program that is free to use. It's great for beginners, has plenty of features for making a good, stable production and can introduce you to the basics of video editing without any financial investments.

Corel VideoStudio Pro:

Price: 54.99

OS: Windows

Corel is an excellent beginner editing software. It offers a ton of features, such as accelerated rendering which makes for faster video creation. Best of all, it has the ability to export videos to YouTube, which saves you valuable time. At such a low price, it's a great entry point into the video editing world.

Medium Budget Options:

Final Cut Pro:

Price: 299.99

OS: Windows

Final Cut Pro is one of the most famous names in the video editing world. Considered to be one of the best editing programs out there, Final Cut Pro offers everything you need for video editing, from start to finish.

Adobe Premiere Pro:

Price: 239.88/yr

OS: Both

Adobe Premiere Pro is the main competitor to Final Cut Pro. It has plenty of options, frequent updates and is perfect for those who are looking for serious editing software. However, one of the more significant drawbacks to Adobe Premier is the fact that their pricing model is monthly or annually. This means that you will always be paying for a subscription to Adobe Premier. When contrasted with Final Cut Pro, which has a one-time flat fee, this renders Adobe significantly more expensive.

However, at the same time, you don't have a high budget to make a lump payment, you can subscribe to Adobe Premier and pay $30.00 a month to use their service. Over time, this will end up costing more than just outright purchasing it, but only if you plan on subscribing for multiple months at a time. It's possible just to drop it, resubscribing only when you need to use it.

While there are other higher priced editing programs out there, Adobe Premier and Final Cut are the two that can be considered industry standard. If you have the budget for one of these, you'd be better off learning how to use one or the other. They have exceptional support and aren't terribly different from each other in terms of features. For the most part, they are so sharply competing with each other that they will always force the other to rise in quality.

Chapter 12: The Mindset to Become a YouTube star

The road to finding real success on YouTube isn't an easy one. If you want to become a YouTube star, you're going to need to embrace the necessary mindset to find that success. While there are plenty of examples of YouTubers who have become famous, the truth is that most of these people didn't achieve their fame overnight. Instead, they spent time and time again, working on their craft, perfecting their art and putting in the hours until finally, they accumulated enough of a following to propel them to the top of the charts.

Is it really possible to achieve that level of success? Absolutely. Is it worth it? Well, that depends on your goals. If you're just using YouTube as a part of your business and marketing efforts, then the time and energy required to reach the top will hinder your other business efforts. Likewise, if you're approaching

YouTube on a hobbyist level, you won't be able to make it to the top. If you want to become a YouTube star, you must treat it with the utmost seriousness that you would any other career choice.

This may, at first, seem a bit extreme. After all, aren't most YouTubers young people who have just accidentally created a giant fanbase? While it may seem like that on the outside, the truth is that most of these YouTubers are serious entrepreneurs who have been able to figure out how to create proper success through hard work and determination. Let's take a look at a few mindsets that are necessary to reach the top of the YouTube world.

Mindset One: Passion

The reason why most of the big YouTubers ended up in a high position is that they are genuinely passionate about what they do. They allow for their passions to spill over into the content they create and as others find out about this content, they respond in kind.

If you want to find long-lasting success on YouTube, you must choose a niche that you are genuinely passionate about. This will aid you immensely in creating the right kind of content for that genre. On top of that, since you are passionate, you will find the work rewarding, thus spurring you on to do more and more.

Don't make the mistake of trying to create content that you think will be popular, just for the sake of getting views. This is often quite inauthentic and will usually result in dry, dull or tryhard videos that most people won't care for. Instead, create the stuff that you enjoy to create. The beauty of the internet is that there is such a wide amount of people online, so don't worry about trying to create content that has mass appeal. The content that you love to create will attract likeminded people, and this will allow you to build a following.

Mindset Two: Focus

Passion alone won't win you any awards. In order to achieve success, you need to have a laser-like focus on the task at hand. The principles of finding success online are relatively simple, really. Create content, generate buzz and engage with fans. Those are the three simple steps necessary to gain a fanbase. However, without focus and discipline, aspiring YouTubers end up neglecting one or more of these three ideas.

You have to stay focused. Create a plan of expansion, create a content schedule and then stick with it. Relentlessly create content, work on advertising for your shows and then engage with commentators and fans. It's easy to get really excited about something, work on it for a few weeks and then slow down once the excitement wears off. Most folks tend to grow frustrated now that their work isn't exciting them anymore and then move onto something else. Maybe they try a new video channel, or perhaps they leave YouTube altogether.

You must be able to endure past the Honeymoon Phase. All projects are fun and exciting when you first start out. But what separates the wheat from the chaff is when the honeymoon is over, and it becomes less exciting to work on the project. This is the most pivotal time, and it requires focus to overcome. If you can push past that barrier, you will find that you will become far more successful than if you only rely on the times that you are excited to work.

Mindset Three: Consistency

If you want to be successful, you need to do more than simply be passionate and focused. You also need to be consistent in your releases. Content releases are extremely important to grow your brand and your channel. You must be willing to put in as much time as possible in creating videos and releasing them on time every week. If you don't, you may end up losing the momentum from the following that you have.

Consistent signals to viewers that you are dedicated to your channel. It will increase your viewing time by quite a bit, which in turn will be rewarded by YouTube's algorithms. And the benefit of having such a steady release schedule is that your backlog will continue to grow and grow. This will aid in increasing your viewing times whenever a new follower decides to go through your backlog.

Mindset Four: Patience

The last mindset to achieving real success in the YouTube world is patience. The fact is, outside of a few rare cases, no one gets famous overnight. Sure, someone might go viral and get a few million views, but there is simply no way to guarantee that will ever happen to you.

If you aren't seeing major results right away, don't be discouraged. It will take quite a bit of time for you to catch your stride. Each hour that you spend will eventually pay off; you just need to be patient. It takes ten years to make an overnight success. This may seem somewhat discouraging at first, but the fact is, if you want to have what it takes to get to the top then you need to be able to keep pushing, no matter how long it's taking.

Those who look for quick and easy stardom, those who wish that all it took was just a few clever videos in order to find success are the ones who often end up falling behind. It's not easy to get to the top; if it were, everyone would be there. You must stay patient and keep at it, no matter what.

Chapter 13: Instagram Essentials

Facebook is an excellent general platform; YouTube is highly specific for content creators. So where does that leave Instagram? Instagram is a powerful platform for sharing and creating visual content. Pictures, short videos, and stories are all a major part of Instagram.

One advantage that Instagram has over the other platforms is that they tend to have a younger audience. On top of that, Instagram users often feel a closer connection with influencers, because they have such close access to the lives of the Instagram poster. When posting on Instagram, you're sharing pictures of your life, often creating narratives about the world that you live in.

Many Instagram influencers show pictures of them living a wonderful life, going on tours in exotic places, taking beautiful pictures of food and hotels. A lot of their followers get a sense of vicarious enjoyment, as they are unable to afford to have such a lifestyle themselves. Over the course of following an influencer, these users tend to develop trust and admiration for the influencer. And if an influencer pitches a specific product, many of their followers will quickly purchase it.

This has led to the creation of what is known as the Instagram Influencer market, where businesses can hire influencers to create strategic sponsorships, all for the purpose of promoting their own products. Influencer marketing is one of the most effective forms of marketing, as followers tend to have a much higher level of trust. This trust and credibility allow them to accept the merits and value of the product.

People trust influencer endorsements significantly more than they do any other kind of endorsement, including celebrity. Why is this? Because celebrity endorsements tend to be perceived as simply paid for gigs. Those endorsements used to be larger in the past, but now, they are regarded as little more than transactional.

All of this is to say that the power and influence that Instagram can provide is quite high. It is possible for you to become an influencer of sorts, at least within your own niche community. While some Influencers have been able to establish their livelihood purely off of sponsorships and to sell their own brands, that's not going to be the scope of these next few chapters. Rather, we're going to be discussing how you can grow your own company's brand to become a strong, authoritative voice in your community.

By growing your influence through Instagram, you'll be able to establish yourself as a credible business. You may even be able to work to establish yourself as a leader in your chosen field. This type of success is possible, but you will need to put in the time and energy to reach that level. Let's talk about some of the basic ideas that work best with Instagram.

Intimacy:

Instagram is intimate in a way that other social media outlets are not. By intimate, we don't mean romantic, but rather we mean close. Instagram gives you the ability to share photos to your followers, complete with captions, descriptions, and hashtags. Many influencers have learned to share close, honest details with their followers. By sharing more in-depth details, by giving people a look on the inside of an influencer's mind and heart, it creates a stronger sense of connection.

Part of that intimacy comes from the storytelling power of pictures. As they say, a picture is worth a thousand words. The right image can strike a strong emotional tone that provokes a response from the viewer. When paired with the proper words, a viewer can experience a window into the mind and heart of the influencer.

Now, as a business, you may be wondering how that intimacy can be used as an advantage. Well, consider the nature of how people relate to giant corporations. For the most part, a corporation is viewed as a faceless entity that has only one interest: making as much money as possible. People tolerate corporations only for the fact that they provide good and services that consumers want. But for the most part, there isn't much of a relationship between individuals and these giant corporations.

As a small business, you have the ability to create an actual relationship with your customers through outlets like Instagram. By sharing behind the scenes photos, a slice of life pictures and other things that aren't focused on direct selling, you are giving people a sense that your company is run by actual human beings.

The intimacy provided by Instagram is good for business. It will let people see your company for more than the products that it sells. You will be able to create relationships with your consumers and in the end, that will add more to your brand authority than anything else.

Hashtags:

While Facebook and YouTube downplay the value of hashtags, Instagram is still going strong with them in 2019. A hashtag is a quick and easy way to categorize information. People primarily search through Instagram by looking up hashtags. Tags that have grown popular will spread, inspiring others to begin using those hashtags themselves. This will increase the search results of a hashtag, which in turn can increase the chances of a user or post being discovered organically.

If you want to find success as an Instagram user, you're going to need to have mastery over the hashtag system. You'll want to learn how to use hashtags properly, when to incorporate them into your posts and how to avoid misusing them. Let's look at a few pointers on how you can use hashtags to maximize your exposure on Instagram.

Hashtag Tip One: Use Established Hashtags

When you're first starting out on Instagram, you won't have much influence. So creating your own hashtags won't do much. You don't have enough followers to make the hashtag popular enough for it to show up in the trending areas. If that's the case, then no one will know to search for your hashtag, meaning it will go virtually unnoticed.

Instead of creating your own hashtags at the beginning, you're going to want to look for relevant, important hashtags that match the type of content you are releasing. Look for hashtags that are trending, that are popular and then find a way to incorporate them int your content. Then, as users search for those hashtags, there is a chance they will organically come across your posts. This increases the chance of gaining them as a follower.

Hashtag Tip Two: Stay Relevant

When it comes to using hashtags, you want to avoid simply stuffing as many as you can into one post. Rather, you should work to include only the hashtags that are relevant to your post. Why? Because you don't want to bring people to your posts under false pretenses. First off, most people can see what your post is just from looking at the search bar. If it doesn't match the hashtag they are searching for; chances are they will just gloss over it. Second, if they do click on your post and find there is nothing relevant to them, they won't stick around and look at more.

Keep your hashtags relevant. Don't include hashtags that have nothing to do with your post, just because that subject is popular.

People will see right through the ruse and will ignore your posts.

Hashtag Tip Three: Use plenty of tags

While the hashtags that you use must be relevant to the post in some way, this doesn't mean you can't have a lot of hashtags. In fact, it's been shown that the more hashtags that you have, the better chance you have of receiving some kind of engagement with others. So don't hold back when it comes to using hashtags. The maximum limit of hashtags that a post can contain is 30, but we'd recommend somewhere between five to ten. This will expand your audience and can increase the chances of getting interaction and follows.

Hashtag Tip Four: Use research tools

Research is an important part of being able to determine the value of the hashtags you are using. It's not a guessing game; you don't have to throw tags out and hope for the best. Instead, you can use research tools, such as

Hashtagify to perform important research on these hashtags. You can see how specific tags are trending, what is currently popular and other important factors for your hashtag. By using these research tools, you can craft well-made posts that will bring in a higher level of followers.

Engagement:

While all social media is based on engagement, Instagram has a closer person to person feel than other platforms. So when someone replies to you, makes a comment or otherwise interacts with your posts, you should work to respond to them. This is an opportunity to engage with your followers, to get to know them better and more importantly, to make a good impression on them. You should make it a point to engage with anyone who communicates with you, provided they are earnest in their interaction. Like our discussion on the YouTube trolls in the previous section, you shouldn't engage with trolls on any platform.

Understanding the Link:

While at the end of the day, the purpose of any business social media page is meant to promote your products and services, Instagram has a different policy than other platforms. They don't allow for linking to outside websites in their posts. Instead, you are given one link, and that is the link on your profile. That's it. You can't link other people to your content outside of that one link.

This changes the purpose of using Instagram. Since you cannot directly provide links to others, you must give them a reason to investigate your profile page and click on your link. This means that over time, people will organically decide to click on your link once you have made a connection with them.

Since you only have the one link to place on your profile, make sure that it is the most relevant link to your business or service. Usually, this will be the homepage to your website.

Brand Awareness:

As we've discussed in the Facebook section, awareness is one of the most necessary steps to creating a sales funnel. You have to be able to generate enough awareness in a customer so that they feel motivated to investigate your products on a closer level. Few platforms make for better awareness of developing engines than Instagram.

The nature of Instagram uses pictures as the primary means of communication. As a brand, you have a unique logo, letterhead, and color scheme. You should work to incorporate these three things into your posts. You don't have to be overt, and you certainly don't need to pitch your products in every post, but by using the same brand identity with each post, you are helping to increase awareness in others.

Over time, individuals who have come to enjoy your posts may end up coming across an ad that is directly selling one of your products. Since you are using the same brand identity in the ad, they will feel more familiar with the ad, and since they have a high level of awareness already, they may become more motivated to look into your ad.

The biggest value that Instagram provides is the ability to generate awareness over time. As long as you work to make thoughtful and interesting posts, stay on message and keep posting, you will be able to introduce your followers to your brand identity over and over again. This can translate into some big sales later on.

Chapter 14: Engaging Followers

As we mentioned in the previous chapter, engagement is one of the most necessary things for success in Instagram. People, by nature, want to get to know each other on some deeper level. Let's talk about some different ways that you can engage with your followers.

Know Your Followers:

It's important that you don't look at your followers as just numbers. Each person who follows you is a real human being, with wants, hopes, interests, and dreams. Spend some time to get to know these people. This doesn't mean that you have to learn about each person who follows you, especially if you end up having hundreds of followers. Rather, you should at least make an effort to understand why these people are following you. Are they interested in your product or the posts that you are making? What motivated them to follow you correctly?

Answering these questions isn't absolutely necessary to find success on Instagram, but it can be helpful for you. It can give you a clear picture of what your followers are looking for. You can make adjustments to the types of posts and content that you create based on what your followers are looking for.

Make a habit to at least try and get a snapshot of what your followers are primarily focused on. You can do this by either going through their profiles and looking at what they engage with the most or creating a composite based on the type of engagement your posts receive. You can also ask them what motivates them to follow you. There's no better market research than just getting a straight answer from the consumer themselves.

Start Conversations

The easiest way to engage those who are following you is to start a conversation. Ask a question and see what results from it. You can ask a serious question, one that prompts thoughtful and curious discussion, or you can just ask a silly, get-to-know-you kind of questions.

The best conversation starters are the ones that provoke positive responses and memories. You don't want to end up asking questions that will start a flame war between followers. You also don't want to ask questions that are too directly related to your products. People will just look at it as a feeble attempt to sell your brand to them. Instead, just be authentic and honest.

Comment on Other's Posts

A great way to create engagement is to be the first person to engage. Instead of waiting for other people to comment on your own posts, you should go out and find other interesting, relevant posts to comment on. As long as you keep these comments positive and kind, you will be able to start conversations with followers who might not be familiar with your brand. You may even end up getting more followers, as you've been engaging with content that belongs to others.

There's nothing wrong with commenting and joining a discussion on a competitor's post, as long as you are able to stay respectful. Don't try to promote yourself or talk down the competition. Instead, just join the conversation and see where the discussion takes you. This is a great way to show that you are more than just a company, but rather a person who actually cares about more than their own product.

Reply Quickly:

When a person is engaging on Instagram and mentions you, you should be quick to visit and reply to them. Even if you are just saying hello or thanks for the mention, it's valuable to move when others are talking to you. If you reply quickly, it makes the user feel as if they have been heard and this, in turn, creates a stronger sense of connection. Conversely, if someone sends you a message, mentions you or comments on your posts and you never get back to them, they might feel ignored and disconnected. You'll want to be able to reply as quickly as possible, to avoid this problem.

Mention Relevant Users

Instagram has a mentioned feature that allows for you to @ an Instagram user in a comment or caption. When you mention them, they will receive a notification that they have been mentioned. This may draw them into the conversation.

Mentions can be useful, especially when mentioning an established brand or influencer. While you don't want to mention people for no reason, there is nothing wrong with mentioning as a method of referring your followers to them. In some cases, this can catch the attention of the person you mentioned, and they may repay the favor later. In either case, make sure that when you mention that you are mentioning only people who have public personas or are already relevant to the conversation at hand. There's no reason to start mentioning people who aren't a part of the conversation or don't have public personas. You won't suddenly attract people to follow and engage with you just because you mentioned them.

Craft Captions:

While it is true that Instagram is heavily focused on visual content, that doesn't mean there is no room for words. Instagram captions are extremely important for creating engagement because it helps the viewer get an understanding of what you are trying to convey with your picture. On top of that, Instagram's algorithms actually view more extended captions in a more positive light, meaning that if you have a long caption, you increase your chances of followers seeing your post.

So what makes for a good caption? Let's take a look at a few things that you can do to make for the best possible Instagram Captions.

Caption Tip One: Provide Context

A picture by itself can be interesting but also provokes curiosity. While some photos speak for themselves, most people want to know more about whatever it is that they're looking at. You can use the caption as an opportunity to provide context for the viewer. Go into detail, share the backstory of how you came to take the picture, why you are sharing it, what makes it so important, etc. These details will increase the chances of a user interacting with your post and engaging with you.

Caption Tip Two: Don't Limit Yourself

If you have a lot to share, then share it! Instagram has a much more generous character limit than other platforms; they allow for up to 2,200 characters per post. This is more than enough for you to share everything that you want to in your post. Of course, you'll need to be disciplined in your writings and make sure that you don't ramble endlessly and that you stay on topic. But if you're worried about being held back by a character limit, don't be. You can share a great deal of information in 2,200 characters.

Caption Tip Three: Build a hook

Just like any kind of written content, you will want to write a hook that will pull readers straight into your caption. If you have a post that contains more than four lines of words, a read more button will be placed on the post, allowing users to expand your post. However, you've got to be able to motivate them to click on the read more button.

The best way to do this is to put your best content at the front and write a line that instantly draws readers in. Don't use clickbaity titles or use tricks to mislead readers, as this will only cause frustration. Instead, just try to come up with a punchy first line that will make a reader interested enough to click on the "more" button.

Caption Tip Four: Format your caption

A caption can be treated as a quick and easy post, or you can expound, going into as much detail as a miniblog. If you've decided to take full advantage of the word limit, you'll need to make sure that you format the captions, so that is highly readable. Nothing can cause a reader to lose interest faster than a lousy format or worse, a wall of text.

Instead, try to break up thoughts with spaces in between. If you make lists, use blank spaces to create a line in between each list item and format them like a bullet point presentation. Just do everything in your power to make sure that the caption looks good and is presentable. The last thing you want is for a great, well-crafted post to end up ignored because the formatting was abysmal.

Hashtags should also go on the bottom of the post, not the top, especially if you have a long string of them. No one wants to have to read their way through five or six hashtags in order to get to the content. Rather, you should include the hashtags at the bottom, once you have finished sharing your thoughts and ideas.

Caption Tip Five: Have a call to action

A great caption often has some kind of call to action within it. Whether the call to action is simply to answer a question you've asked or to visit your bio, if you want to motivate people, you need to direct them towards something. The call to action doesn't need to be in every single post that you make, but it should be in the captions that you have crafted for the purpose of moving your brand forward in some way.

Caption Tip Six: Don't be afraid of Emojis

While many people can knock emojis because they seem silly, the truth is that most Instagram users prefer to use Emojis. An emoji can convey an idea or emotion rather quickly and most importantly, can break up the monotony of your post. Colorful, fun emojis scattered here and there, throughout the post will keep things light and make for an easy read.

Of course, you'll want to make sure you practice moderation with your emojis. Don't go overboard and try to post them in between every few words. Instead, try to treat them as exclamation points, you should use them here and there, but not on every sentence.

Caption Tip Seven: Don't rush the caption out

A carefully crafted caption can make all the difference for your Instagram account. It can increase engagement, drive likes and bring in new followers. More importantly, it can even direct people to your bio, where the link resides. All of these rewards can make people feel a little hasty and so they'll rush to create a caption as quickly as possible.

However, creating a good caption isn't about speed. While other sites like Twitter encourage users to put out their ideas quickly, you have much more room to write here. This means you should treat your task of writing a caption quite seriously. Take your time in writing it. Work on it in multiple drafts, making sure that no words are wasted. You don't want to write a caption as much as you want to craft one. Then, once you're ready to release it, you will be putting out a high-quality caption that will drive significantly more engagement than a first draft that was slapped together in five minutes.

Chapter 15: Instagram Stories

Marketing is, in a big way, a form of storytelling. You want people to be able to tap into ideas that are bigger than "buy my product." You want them to feel as if they are a part of something, something important, something that matters. When you are able to pull a reader into your stories, you help move them closer to your brand identity.

Instagram is one of the best platforms for this type of storytelling. Instagram Stories is a feature that allows users to create videos and posts that exist only for 24 hours. After the twenty-four hour period expires, the video vanishes forever.

This might seem strange from a content creation point of view, as most content creators want to have their work exist for more than just a day. However, the point of Instagram Stories isn't to create content, but rather an *experience*. Since you only get to participate in an Instagram story during a brief period of time, you are experiencing something that is relatively unique. Those who didn't have a chance to watch the story have missed out on something that will never come back.

So what is the advantage of a business using Instagram Stories? Well, the first and perhaps the biggest is that you don't have the ability to doctor up an Instagram Story. Instagram only uses content that was recorded in the last 24 hours through their app, meaning that you can't upload some carefully produced video. Rather, businesses have the ability to share raw, honest videos about their world.

This can create a tremendous advantage when it comes to the creation of behind the scenes videos. Instead of giving viewers the polished, finished production of a BTS, users will be able to see things as they really are. This can give viewers a better sense of how authentic the company is actually being.

And behind the scenes is just the beginning when it comes to Instagram Stories. Let's take a look at all the exciting ways that a business can take advantage of Instagram Stories!

Create Polls:

Instagram Stories allows for an option to create polls for users. All you need to do is create a story post and then select the poll option. This then lets you create a question with two response fields. Then, when your Story goes live, your viewers will be able to watch and interact with the poll, giving their answers.

Not only is this a great way to aggregate information about your customers, but it can also be entertaining for users. Don't just stick to asking serious business questions; rather, ask interesting and curious questions that will provoke a response from them in some way.

Then, once you have finished the poll, you can post an additional story the next day, sharing the results of the poll and then perhaps giving some kind of additional information. Really, the potential for how you use these poll is limitless. As long as you keep them fun and interesting, viewers will enjoy taking them from time to time!

Countdowns:

If you're preparing for an announcement or a product release, then you might want to consider using Instagram Stories to create a countdown. To create a countdown, you just need to attach a countdown sticker to your post. Once the countdown is running, viewers can click on it to subscribe to the event that they are waiting for. Then, when the countdown reaches 0, it will notify all the subscribers and let them know that the countdown has completed. This, of course, will prompt them to visit your stories to see what the big exciting news is about.

Countdowns are a great way to build hype around anything. They work best when you are able to keep the announcement news shrouded in mystery. Building a campaign that gives hints and ideas about what the announcement could be, leading up to the countdown is a great way to increase that hype. Then, once the countdown is finished, share the news and watch the reaction spread!

Giveaways:

Another great way to generate buzz and excitement over your products is to run a giveaway through your Instagram Story. Since the giveaway will only last for the life of the story, which is 24 hours, it will increase engagement from viewers.

Most giveaways on Instagram require some kind of action on the part of the viewers. The most common type of giveaway is a comment giveaway, where all a person needs to do in order to win is comment on a post. Then after the time period is over, you randomly select a winner and then inform them via DM.

Other types of giveaways include getting photos from users who are doing a specific activity, making their own Instagram stories or even taking some kind of action off the platform, such as signing up with Gleam.io for the giveaway.

Regardless of the type of giveaway that you choose, make sure that you are following Instagram's rules for promotion. For the most part, there aren't many restrictions other than following the local laws about giveaways, but there is one important rule that they enforce. Per their guidelines "*You must not inaccurately tag content or encourage users to inaccurately tag content (example: don't encourage people to tag themselves in photos if they aren't in the photo).*" Other than that, you're good to go.

Giveaways generate buzz, brand awareness and most importantly, excitement for the products you are giving away. If someone really wants that product and is willing to enter a contest, they might just want it badly enough to buy it later on. Sometimes people may not even become aware of a product's existence until they hear about a contest giving it away.

The only costs that you incur with an Instagram giveaway are the cost of the products you are giving away for free. And in truth, you will most likely be able to recoup those losses from the amount of buzz generated by your giveaway.

Announcements:

If you have a big announcement to make, you might want to consider using an Instagram Story to let your followers on Instagram know first. While you wouldn't want to solely focus on using short-lived media as a means of keeping your followers informed about your companies comings and goings, you can use Stories as a way to give them insider knowledge. Sure, you'll go public with the announcement on your blog or other social media platforms, but if you share these announcements with your followers first, it can generate more buzz that way.

On top of that, if you're selling products or services that have only a limited amount of stock or slots, you are rewarding your followers by giving them access to this information first. That means they can jump on the train early and make purchases or pre-orders before others. In a lot of ways, this helps to turn your Instagram feed into more of a club for your fans. Those who will want to get in on that club will simply have to follow you, which in turn increases the number of fans and followers that you have.

Flash Deals:

Another great function of the 24-hour time limit is that you are able to run quick, short-lived promotions. A flash deal on a product that is only available for a limited amount of time can drive a high level of traffic and more importantly, can also drive conversions. If a follower has been sitting on the fence about purchasing one of your products for a while, but suddenly has 24 hours to get the product for 20% off, they very well might convert.

The value of a flash deal is twofold. It can drive up conversions, but it also creates an incentive for your followers to pay attention to your stories. Since you can't see a story without being inside of it, this will create an incentive for your followers to watch your stories more often. After all, if they are enjoying your products, they might be excited at the prospect of being able to get in on a flash deal.

A word of caution, however. Sales, like all things, should be done in moderation. The last thing you want is for your customers to be burned out because you are keeping running sales every single day. Instead, try to keep a limit to your flash deals to every now and then. Don't run them enough to where your followers get frustrated at yet another deal. This will reduce fatigue and increase the chances of actually receiving conversions when you run these deals.

Just For Fun:

It's important to remember that Instagram stories aren't solely about ruthlessly marketing to your followers. They expect to see content that is enjoyable, fun and to their benefit. While certain types of Stories, such as giveaways and sales are great for growing your business, they can't be the backbone of the content that you are generating.

The majority of what you want to share should be designed to provide entertainment, education or inspiration to your followers. This is the type of content and experiences that will help keep a follower coming back to your stories, time and time again. If they begin to feel that you are making these stories purely for the purpose of marketing, they're most likely going to stop watching them. Worse yet, they may even end up unfollowing you.

So have fun with the stories that you are creating. Try to tell actual stories, give behinds the scenes that show the humanity and comedy of your organization. Show breathtaking videos of views that you experience. Do anything you can to help your viewers see your brand in a personal manner. This will give you credibility, establish a healthy rapport and keep them visiting your stories time and time again. Remember, the 80/20 rule applies across the board, and that includes Instagram!

Chapter 16: Instagram Ads

Instagram is owned by Facebook, which means that if you want to run ads on Instagram, you'll need to go through the Facebook Ads manager. The good news here is that since they are both related, all of the work that you put into developing a strong custom audience for your Facebook marketing efforts can also be used on your Instagram efforts!

Instagram offers several different types of ads, ranging from static images to story ads, to videos and even to carousel ads. These different ad types provide you with different options (and costs) which will allow you to get the very best out of the advertising experience.

What makes Instagram ads so crucial is the fact that Instagram restricts you to only one link. However, when you're running ads through Instagram, you are free to link people to your products and web pages as much as you like. In addition to that, some Instagram ads have features that allow viewers to actually make a purchase from inside the app, which can quickly move a customer through your sales funnel at a rapid pace!

For the most part, creating an Instagram ad is the exact same as creating a Facebook ad. In fact, you can even run both ads at the same time, allowing Facebook to run your ad on both platforms with a simple check of a box. When an ad is being run, the Instagram ad will simply appear in the feed of the users as they are scrolling through.

However, there is one type of ad that is different from all the others on Instagram: the Story Ad. The Story ad doesn't show up in the ad feed, but rather it shows up in between stories for users. For example, if a viewer is watching several stories, flicking through each one, an ad will appear in the middle, breaking up the viewing experience for a short period of time. It is there that your story ad will play.

There is tremendous value behind the story ad, simply for the fact that most viewers are fairly engaged with what they are watching. As they switch to another story, they will be a captive audience for a short period of time, allowing you to get your advertisement in front of them. Best of all, they don't have the option to skip the ad. You will have their total attention, but only for a very brief time. Let's go take a look at the ways that you can craft an effective Instagram Story Ad.

Take Full Advantage of Production:

While Instagram Stories are meant to be unpolished, spur of the moment type of videos with minimal editing, Story Ads are entirely different. You have the luxury of spending time creating the best possible ad for your business. This means you'll want to embrace the fact that you can actually work to create a well-produced video.

This, of course, costs time and money. While it is possible for you to create cheap and fun Instagram Story ads, the truth is that production value does matter. Clever writing, good camera work, and good editing can work wonders for your brand. On the flipside, if you don't have quality in your ad, you end up risking the chance of your target demographic ignoring the ad entirely – quality matters.

Catch Attention Quickly:

Just because a viewer has to sit through your video before they are able to get to the next Instagram story doesn't mean that they have to pay attention. It's easy to look away from an ad, or even to simply close out of the app if they are that bored. You'll need to make sure that your video is able to capture their attention as soon as possible. This requires snappy direction, witty writing, and strong visuals. Work to make your story pop out. Have a strong hook that will turn their heads.

The good news is that since you're using a targeted advertising system, the people your ads will be in front of are already part of your relevant audience. However, just because you know that your ad or product will be relevant to their interests doesn't mean you can neglect to capture attention. People see hundreds of ads a day; you must work to capture their attention and then let your product relevance entice them to click through the ad.

Create a Strong Call to Action:

Since you're running an advertisement that will cost you money, you're going to want to make sure that you have an active call to action in your ad. This call to action should have some kind of urgency, some kind of motivating factor that will push viewers towards clicking on your ad. Coming up with a limited time offer, or a special price for those who click now is a great way to move them through your funnel.

Whatever you choose your call to action to be, the next steps should be made clear to them. They should know what to do next, be it click on the link, follow you on Instagram or visit another website. You should give them a clear set of instructions at the end of the commercial if you're running an ad that is primarily focused on generating conversions.

Use Boomerangs:

One type of video that is popular is what's known as a Boomerang. The Boomerang app takes a regular video and then breaks it down into ten separate photos. Then, it runs through all the photos at speed making the photos appear to be moving as if it were a stop motion film. This effect is pretty popular with those who use Instagram as well as advertisers. Why? Because this stop motion effect is perceived as cute, light and whimsical.

To create a boomerang, you'll need to download the actual app and then select which video you want to use. From there, the app will do the rest, creating the perfect video for you to then use for your story ad.

Should you use a Boomerang for your video? If you're trying to keep things simple, demonstrate a product or idea and you don't have sound, this can add a lot of charm and production value to an otherwise normal video. Feel free to play with it and experiment, see if using boomerangs is right for your product. Sometimes they can look great, especially if the video is of something mundane, such as a box being opened. Other times, they might not fit, especially if you're trying to create a more action-oriented video. It's just another tool to have in the toolbox.

Use Music:

Music can be crucial in creating emotional responses in viewers. It sets the mood, informs the viewer of what the tone of the ad will be and most importantly, it will help create an emotional connection between the viewer and the product.

That being said, there are a lot of potential issues that can spring up from using music. The biggest one is licensing. If you want to use music, you're going to need to have the legal rights to use that music in your ad, or else it could get unlisted. However, finding music to use for commercial purposes is fairly easy to do; all you need is to spend some time searching online for companies that sell commercial use licenses. These often cost a flat fee and then you are able to use that music for your own purposes.

In general, you want the music to match the objective of your ad. If you want to create a sense of wonder and mystique, you'll want to use music that is slow and ponderous. If you want to create a sense of delight and happiness, then upbeat, ukelele type music often works best. Regardless, you'll want the music to complement and work with the ad, not to distract the viewers.

Use Comedy:

Humor is an extremely potent tool. Since you don't have a tremendous amount of time to make an impact on the viewer, a great way to keep their attention is to make them laugh. A quick joke, a surreal scene or making light of your own product can be a great way to put a customer in a good mood. Showing that you have a sense of humor and that you don't take yourself too seriously can help motivate the viewer to click through, perhaps in the hopes of finding more of that humor on your website.

There are limitations to humor, of course. Not everyone finds the same things to be funny, and certain products can be difficult to make jokes about. But at the same time, if you write a funny enough sketch, it may end up striking a chord with the viewer, and they could potentially share it with others. That could translate into generating more awareness, especially if you have viewers telling others about the funny commercial that they saw.

Have a Clear Brand:

One of the most crucial parts of running an ad on any platform is your brand identity. A customer needs to be able to identify that your ad is part of your brand almost immediately. This comes from the integration of your logo, as well as using the same font and colors as your brand identity. The logo doesn't need to be overpowering, or even the centerpiece of the ad, but it does need to be present so that viewers will come to associate those products with your company.

Keep the Ad Tight and Focused:

The phrase "less is more" exists for a reason. Sometimes, when creating an ad, we can become overwhelmed with the number of possibilities. In some cases, we may even end up trying to pack too much into a single ad. This can possibly torpedo your ad if you aren't careful. Rather than try to incorporate a bunch of different ideas into one ad, try to stick to one idea at a time.

Develop the overall theme and purpose of your ad first. Are you creating a lighthearted ad for the purpose of getting a conversion? Is it a mysterious and soundless ad, meant to raise awareness? Once you have been able to determine what your theme and purpose is, then you can go to the drawing board and start working on ideas. Make sure that every idea that you come up with fits that purpose and that theme.

When it comes to the brainstorming phase, there is often no shortage of ideas. However, you can't run with everything, so make a point to limit yourself. Keep your ad tight and focused on conveying the one unique idea you are trying to get across. If you find yourself with multiple good ideas, try to break them up into their own separate ads instead of just jamming them all together. This will give you a higher level of variety for your ads as well as keep your ads clean and comfortable to view.

Conclusion:

Social media marketing is one of the most important ways that a business can grow. We've covered three different platforms, Facebook, YouTube, and Instagram, sharing the ways you can grow on each one. Regardless of the platform that you choose to work with, whether it's just one or a mix of all three, the principles of good social media practice are the same. Focus on creating value for your followers, don't spend too much time talking about yourself, and above all, be authentic with others. The more connections that you are able to make, the more you'll be able to grow your business. Good luck out there!